Spearfishing

How to Get Started

Doug Peterson

Copyright © 2013 Doug Peterson

All rights reserved.

ISBN: 1494705796
ISBN-13: 978-1494705794

Contents

Introduction 1
   The purpose of this book 1
   How I Got Involved 3
   The very basic premise of spearfishing – one man's perspective 6
Chapter 1 – Basic Training 8
   Giving in to the pressure 8
   Taking a SCUBA certification course 11
   Pressure and Equalizing 13
   Safety Matters 1: Diving with a head cold 15
   Buoyancy Control 16
   Safety Matters 2: The Buddy System 20
Chapter 2 – Basic Equipment 23
   Wetsuits 24
   Weight Systems 30
   Masks 33
   Snorkels 39
   Fins 42
   Speargun 44
   Floatlines 50
   Dive Float 52
   Dive Computer 54
   Other Accessories 55
   Cost of basic equipment 56
      Equipment Cost Estimates 60

Sources for equipment 61
Cleaning and maintenance 62

Chapter 3 – Where to Go Spearfishing 64
Visual cues 65
The bottom of the sea 68

Chapter 4 – Species of Fish 72
Striped Bass 72
Blackfish (Tautog) 75
Fluke (Summer Flounder) 77
Bluefish 79
Porgy (Scup) 81
Triggerfish 82
Other species 83

Chapter 5 – Getting Wet 84
Shore dives 84
Kayak dives 89
Boat Dives 92

Chapter 6 – Freediving and Spearfishing Technique 102
The equipment checklist 102
Loading the speargun 105
Relaxing at the surface 106
Surface breathing 108
   Recovery/Relaxation Breathing Cycle 109
The one big breath 111
   The big breath pathway 113
Pike position 114

Time to start equalizing 115

The descent to the bottom 116

Adjusting weights for buoyancy control 118

Bottom time 119

Out of air – time to come up 121

Warning – The shallow water blackout 124

    Hook Breathing Cycle 125

    Purge Breaths 125

Chapter 7 – Underwater Hunting 127

    A stealthy approach 127

    Stick to the bottom 128

    Line up your shot 129

    Fighting a fish 131

    Reloading 135

        Recovery/Relaxation Breathing Cycle 136

    Keeping a log 136

Chapter 8 - Caring For Your Catch 138

    Ice Bath 138

    Cleaning 140

    Preserving 142

Chapter 9 – Specialty Hunting 143

    Diving at night 143

    Spearfishing at night 149

Chapter 10 – Spearfishing Tournaments 151

Appendix A - Online spearfishing resources 154

Index 155

Disclaimer

Freediving and spearfishing are potentially dangerous and life-threatening activities and are not to be taken lightly. The author of this book is not a professional diver or a certified licensed instructor and assumes no responsibility for the actions of anyone who reads this book.

Introduction

The purpose of this book

The purpose of this book is to provide some basic information to the beginner who is just starting or even thinking about the sport of spearfishing. There is a lot of helpful information that I have acquired mainly through trial and error and I would have really liked a guide like this when I started out. Additionally, I see people from time to time who are just starting out in the sport who do not have the basic training necessary to be safe in the underwater environment. Safety should always come first and although spearfishing can be an extremely rewarding activity, it can also be very dangerous if the basic rules of diving are not followed.

By reading through this book and following my experiences you should be able to get a basic understanding about how to get started in spearfishing. You will learn about the equipment that is necessary as well as other optional equipment that is useful for a variety of situations. Hopefully, I will leave you with enough knowledge that you will feel confident about getting started. In addition, I will include resources for you so that you can go beyond the basics in this sport. I will provide several online sites that can offer a wealth of additional information as well as sites where you can find the right equipment to suit your needs.

I too am still a relative beginner in the world of spearfishing. It has opened up so many new worlds of adventure for me and I hope that by sharing my knowledge and experience that many more people can enter the underwater world with confidence and enthusiasm.

I have two friends that I am going to talk about from time to time. They are Greg and Pete. I met Greg a few years ago. We were friends and played on a softball team together. After getting to know him better, I learned that he enjoyed going fishing just as much as I had. We met up on several occasions to go fishing for striped bass, fluke, squid, trout and we even tried our hand at ice fishing. To be perfectly honest, we both loved fishing for the same reasons – to have an opportunity to catch something really big and bring it home for dinner. But time after time we went fishing and were unsuccessful. It was nice to have someone like Greg to share the experiences with but it would have been so much better if we learned how to be successful. During one of our fishing trips we started to have a discussion about diving and snorkeling and I found out that Greg too had an interest in spearfishing. He just hadn't pursued it to the degree that I had and needed a bit of a jump start. This was a perfect opportunity for both of us. I could teach what I had learned to Greg and Greg could be my dive buddy so we could be as safe as possible. Greg had another friend, Pete, who was also a beginner fisherman and showed an interest in learning spearfishing as well. This turned out to be the best situation of all because three is the ideal number to go on a spearfishing adventure. I will explain why in a later chapter about diving from a boat.

So Greg, Pete and I began a new friendship linked by the desire to learn about freediving, spearfishing, and how to get some fish for dinner. Greg and Pete made many mistakes at first. They needed some guidance about what equipment to have and certain diving techniques. As I get further into this book and start to describe equipment in greater detail, I will show you some of these common mistakes that could have been avoided.

How I Got Involved

I got involved with spearfishing almost by accident but there had always been a curious part of me that wondered what it would be like to swim with the fish that I had been catching – or more accurately, not catching. My journey began when I moved to Rhode Island, a state pretty much surrounded by water and rocky coastline.

I was excited to live in RI. I had always enjoyed fishing with a rod and reel. Fishing became a passion of mine when I was very young and the allure continued whenever I found myself near a body of water. I learned all that I know about fishing from my father who is an avid fly fisherman. My biggest problem, however, was that I think I enjoyed the sport of catching a little bit better than the sport of fishing. As I got older, these feelings intensified and I found out that my main reason for going fishing was really to do some catching! It sounds obvious, I know. But if you closely know, or are one of those die-hard fishermen out there, you can probably attest that the love for fishing and just being outdoors is motivation enough. You know who you are. There are tons of guys and some girls as well but not nearly as many girls, who have this inner pull toward the sea. It's a force that cannot be explained very well (especially by me) that causes them to abandon their families and their lives in the pursuit of a day of fishing. And it's not just once or for a day here and there. It's a lifetime - a lifestyle. It's a lifestyle filled with thousands of trips back and forth from your home to your favorite watering hole. This is a life that many people choose to lead but it is a solitary one. Aside from the friends who have exactly the same life, and the tackle shop owners, it is very difficult to have relationships when you are motivated to be a fisherman. So why do they do it? The one word answer to that question - Hope. A fisherman's best friend is hope. The adventure into the unknown realm of the sea is an exciting one filled with hopes and dreams of landing the big one on any given day. This adventure to the sea temporarily releases the fisherman from all

of his other daily life struggles. "Hope is like the sun, which as we journey toward it casts the shadow of our burdens behind us."
~Samuel Smiles

As any fisherman can attest, every once in a while you have one of those fantastic days – a magical day. It is the day that you will talk about to your friends and family and strangers until the end of time. Literally. It's the story that keeps you traveling back to that same spot over and over and over again, year after year. You have the hope that one day you will be able to relive that magical day and when you do, everything will be right in the world once again. If you're anything like me, you're even thinking about your story right now as you read this. You know you are. You can't help it. Everything went right that day and that's exactly what brings you back and keeps you attracted to the sport of fishing. I'll tell you what also brings you back to that same spot time after time. It's also the failure. That's right – the failure of going back so many times to the spot where the magic happened, yet does not happen again. Strange isn't it? This is the exact same spot. I'm doing the same thing, same time of day, same tide, same lure, same bait, etc. No fish. So we shake off that failure, conveniently forget about it, and try again another day. It happens again and again and your memory of that fantastic day is what keeps bringing you back. You can't fully appreciate the success until you fully know what the failure is like. There can be no good without knowing the evil. You can't have light without first knowing darkness. Blah, blah, blah. . . I think I'm getting a little ahead of myself here. We'll save that for another discussion.

So where was I? Ah, yes. Occasionally, if you put the time in, you have another magical day and then another. Over time this gives you more stories and more secret spots and even more reason to continue your quest to become the nomadic fisherman that doesn't have much of a life outside fishing. Putting the time in is the key and for some of us that is a luxury that we cannot afford. We have families, jobs, responsibilities, etc. I believe I was saying earlier that I like catching quite a bit more than fishing. That's because when I finally do get a window of opportunity in my life to go out and enjoy some time fishing, I want to also have some success at it. Fishing is mysterious enough when you have special spots and past successes and failures. But when you're just a weekender trying to bring an occasional catch home for the dinner table, it would be nice to experience a bit more on the success end. Maybe I was just a terrible fisherman. I don't think so because I really enjoyed it but I certainly found that my failures were outweighing my successes to such a degree that it was starting to get a little depressing. I know fishing is not easy but every once in a while it would have been nice to have one of those magical days. It just wasn't happening for me.

So, through a series of unrelated coincidences, I found myself learning how to become a spearfisherman. I have always had a desire to learn how to SCUBA dive. I've always loved the ocean and have always been a very good swimmer. There were just two things holding me back from learning how to dive. One was the movie Jaws. And the other was the expense. It is a costly sport and even the certification and training can be cost prohibitive for many people – not to mention the expense for equipment. Through some lucky circumstance, I found myself having about $400 of disposable cash (I won it in a nice football pool) with which I decided to fulfill a longtime goal to get dive certified.

I started my training at a local dive shop in Rhode Island. The instructors were die-hard SCUBA guys but a section of the shop was dedicated solely to spearfishing. Because of my interest in fishing I was naturally drawn to this section of the shop and I became very inquisitive about the whole process. The instructors were very willing to share their experiences with me and to help me get started. However, going back one step, I cannot emphasize enough the importance of going through the formal SCUBA dive certification training program before becoming a freediving spearfisher. I will get into more detail in later chapters about why this is so important for safety reasons. For the beginner, this is not a matter to be taken lightly.

And so began my adventure into the sport of spearfishing.

The very basic premise of spearfishing – one man's perspective

When I first began I had the idea in my head that I would gear up, jump into the water and swim around trying to get close enough to the fish in order to shoot them. I went out with Mike, who was my mentor and dive instructor. He watched me flounder around, unsuccessfully chasing fish for a while before letting me in on the secret. If you take nothing else from the knowledge in this book, remember this simple principle. Hold your breath, dive to the bottom and become a rock. Stay there as motionless as possible for as long as you can and the fish will come to you. That's it – and that's the key to success in spearfishing.

Most fish are naturally curious creatures – some species more than others. They know when something is different in their environment and they want to check it out. After all, it could potentially be something to eat. However, they are also naturally nervous creatures. Anything bigger than them will most likely want to eat them so they need this instinctive protective mechanism to survive. If you are swimming around (very non fish like) their nervous instincts will overrule their sense of curiosity and they will keep their distance. If you are a rock, they want to see this strange new rock and will come in for a closer look. With practice you will be able to act like a rock for longer and longer times and your patience will be rewarded.

Also remember this – the formula for success:

Comfort = Less Stress = More Air = More Time = More Fish = More Fun

Keep these basic principles in mind while you read through this book. I will refer back to them from time to time as a reminder.

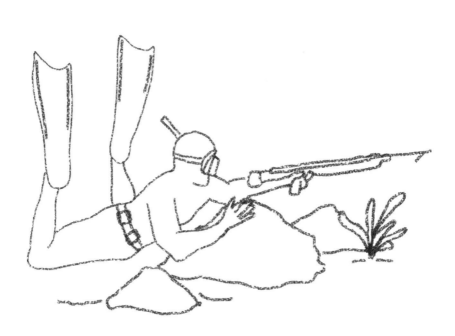

Chapter 1 – Basic Training

Giving in to the pressure

Spearfishing is a sport where the fisherman meets the freediver. Freediving, a sport in itself, in its simplest form means holding your breath and swimming underwater. There are no air tanks, regulators, BCs or artificial breathing apparatuses. It's just you and the water. Hold your breath, dive down deep and come up when you're out of breath. That's it. The first section of this book will be dedicated to teaching you how to become a proficient freediver.

Many of us have excellent freediver training already just from our childhood experiences in swimming pools. Did you ever play the game, 'Who can hold your breath the longest?' with some of your friends? Or 'How far can you swim underwater with one breath?' Both are great for the future freediver. I used to love playing those games. Little did I know that it would be very helpful when I started learning the finer points of spearfishing.

Well, did you ever hold your breath and dive down deep to the bottom of the pool and feel pain in your ears as you approached the bottom? I can remember feeling like my ears were going to explode (or more accurately, implode) as I went deeper and deeper. This feeling also prevented me from going as deep as I really could go. And the pain in my ears prevented me from staying at that depth for any extended period of time. It is very uncomfortable.

This painful feeling is the pressure of a lot of water pushing down on any air spaces in your body. Your head and ears in particular have tiny air spaces that do not like to be "squeezed" because they are surrounded by bone and hard tissue. When you get this squeeze, there is a lot of discomfort involved because the air in the spaces is being compressed into a smaller volume. The air spaces in your head are surrounded by tissue that doesn't like to flex very much and when the air space gets compressed, so does the hard tissue. As you go deeper and deeper under water the pressure gets greater and the air spaces get squeezed more and more until your head actually gets squished from the inside out. This collapse of the air space is an implosion as opposed to an explosion.

You also have air spaces in your lungs and in other organ systems but these structures have more flex or elasticity and do not cause as much discomfort when subjected to the same pressure differences. To give you a clearer understanding of this pressure effect, picture a balloon filled with air floating on the surface of the ocean. If the balloon was pulled underwater the pressure of the water pushing on the surface of the balloon would cause the air inside to be compressed. The balloon would get smaller and smaller as it was pulled deeper and deeper. On a molecular level, the molecules of air inside the balloon are getting tighter and tighter together and. . . ahh – sorry for putting you to sleep with the 'science' behind all of this. I told you this was going to be a basic introduction to spearfishing and now I'm going on and on about molecules and air pressure and science. I'll give myself a slap each time I start rambling so I can get back on track.

Anyway – back to the balloon (that's easier to understand – even kids understand the balloon example). So the same balloon, as you bring it back up to the surface, will start to expand. The pressure of the water gets less and less and the air inside expands the balloon.

Because the balloon is rubber, it easily expands back to its original size without too much stress on it.

What would happen if the balloon was deep underwater and then it was inflated and tied? As it was brought to the surface, the air inside would continue to expand and the balloon would get bigger and bigger until it could not contain the air any longer – boom! Explosion. So, even though the balloon is elastic, there is still only so much air it can contain until something must give.

Let's look at another example. Suppose now you have something a little more rigid than a balloon. A 2 liter plastic soda bottle with the cap on tight. The bottle is a specific shape and size and is not elastic like the balloon. As the bottle is taken underwater, can you imagine the effect that the water pressure has upon it? That's right, it gets squeezed and deformed and bent out of its original shape. The air inside must be compressed and as it is, the bottle cannot shrink in size like the balloon could. The walls of the bottle collapse inward (implode) as it bends and crumples.

Now here's how all of this relates to freediving. Your head is the bottle, and your lungs are the balloon.

Picture the balloon and bottle example again and imagine if you can the fully inflated balloon attached to the bottle so that air can pass between them. Take both the balloon and bottle underwater just like before. Now what happens to the bottle as the water pressure causes the air to compress? If you guessed right, the bottle does not crumple any more. Why? Because as the air compresses inside the bottle, it can now borrow some air from the attached balloon. All of the air is compressed and the balloon shrinks like before and shrinks even more because it has to lend some air to the rigid bottle so that the bottle can retain its shape.

Translating this example to your head and lungs, imagine yourself taking a deep breath (inflating your balloon lungs) and diving underwater. As the water pressure begins to crumple your head (the bottle) you can equalize the pressure by borrowing some air from your lungs. Your elastic lungs will compress a bit but more importantly your head can maintain its original shape and size. Nobody likes a crumpled head. Crumpled head = pain. The word "equalize" is very important here and will be used a lot in later chapters so it is essential that you understand this concept in its basic form.

The balloon and the bottle can now go up and down in the water and the pressure is equalized throughout the system. The concept of pressure and equalizing is one of the most important things a beginning diver must know. To fully grasp how water pressure plays its role here it is imperative that you educate yourself by taking an introductory SCUBA diving course.

Taking a SCUBA certification course

Chances are, if you live anywhere near the water there is a dive shop or a YMCA nearby. If affordable, sign up for a course and spend some time in a classroom setting with a qualified instructor. This is a good first step toward being as safe as possible in the water. There you will learn all of the basic principles about atmospheric pressures, water pressures, and equalizing – all in a controlled environment.

As I said earlier, I was fortunate that my interests brought me to the SCUBA certification training. Not only was I introduced to spearfishing by the instructors there, but I was very well educated in all of the other areas before I even stepped into the water. Can you go freediving and spearfishing without certification? Yes. However, the information that you get at the certification course is invaluable when you begin the journey as a freediver.

SCUBA training and certification is somewhat expensive. I would guess that a proper course would cost in the $300-$450 range. Not to mention the fact that if you want to pursue that type of diving, the equipment costs can be overwhelming for the beginner. If the cost of the SCUBA training is too much for you and you know that you specifically want to learn freediving for the purpose of spearfishing then you may want to approach the dive shop owner with that suggestion. That specific type of training may already be available there. Each shop is different and usually tailored toward the interest of that particular dive shop owner. It doesn't hurt to ask and if they do not instruct for spearfishing purposes then maybe they can suggest another shop that is better suited for you.

If the cost to take a suitable course is still too much for you at this time, then at bare minimum you should invest in and read the PADI Open Water Diver Manual. PADI stands for Professional Association of Dive Instructors and is the authority on all things dive related. Their open water manual comes with the basic training course but even if you don't formally take the course, you can still teach yourself just about everything you need to know by reading that manual. It is very informative and easy to read. It will give you a little more science than I am prepared to offer here but it is written in a way that most children can comprehend very easily.

There was a lot that I got out of my dive training course and open water manual. The most important principles that I took from the course were: Pressure and Equalizing (which I already touched on briefly), Buoyancy control, and the Buddy System. I will spend some more time getting into a little more detail on each of these subjects.

Pressure and Equalizing

Now that you know that you can't go very far underwater without feeling like the squeeze is going to crumple your head, I will now tell you about some basic ways to equalize the pressure in your system. After all, you are a little more complex than a balloon and bottle (I hope) and learning how to use the air in your lungs to equalize the pressure in your head will take a bit of practice.

The main areas that will need to be equalized are your ears and your sinuses. The easiest way for you to equalize all of the air spaces your head is to close your mouth, pinch closed your nose and gradually push the air pressure outward using your lungs and your diaphragm. Do this very slowly at first. You can do it right now so you can see what it feels like. As you gradually push you will create a positive air pressure and you will most likely feel it in your ears in the form of a slight pop. Be very careful not to push too hard and do not continue pushing after your pressure has equalized. To do so could cause some damage to your eardrums so be very careful with this at first and take it slowly.

You've just experienced what it feels like to equalize the pressure in your head and ears. The easiest place to try this out underwater is in a swimming pool. If you have access to a pool, practice this as you dive down to the bottom. You need a pool that has some depth to it. The pressure doesn't start to affect you until you go deeper than about 5-8 feet. The depth may differ from person to person and vary depending on your experience level. When starting to learn this technique you should pinch closed your nose and continually push back some positive pressure as you go deeper. This will give you some idea when your body needs to equalize.

For example, get to about 6 feet and equalize. You will feel a positive pressure release and if you stay at that depth, you should not have any further discomfort. If you continue to descend you will need to equalize again every 6-10 feet or so. The technical term for this depth change is an 'atmosphere.' The atmosphere is explained in more detail in the PADI manual but what you really need to know is that the pressure continues to increase as you go deeper and deeper. And each time you feel the discomfort start in your head and ears, it's time to equalize again. Actually, it is best to equalize just before you start to feel any discomfort. This feeling will come with experience and practice.

The pressure put on your air spaces as you descend is called negative air pressure. The reason why I said that it is best to equalize before you start to feel any discomfort is because the negative pressure can get too strong and you will be unable to equalize. You will push and push and not be able to get relief. This is a very uncomfortable situation. You have to relieve the negative pressure and the only solution is to ascend toward the surface. As you may have guessed, as you swim upward, the pressure lessens and it will get to the point where you will be able to equalize again. If you learn to anticipate the depth when the negative pressure will start to affect you, then you will be able to continually equalize just before these depths. When you can achieve this, it will make diving much more comfortable for you. You have to master this process if you plan to become a proficient spearfisher.

With proper equalizing you should be able to dive as deep as you want to without experiencing the squeeze. When you decide to go back to the surface, the pressure works in the opposite way. You actually feel an automatic pressure release in your ears as you ascend upward. Just let it happen. There is no need to do anything else.

Safety Matters 1: Diving with a head cold

If you have a cold or a sinus infection of any kind, do not attempt to dive. I'm not going to get into too many medical details here but if the air passages in your head are blocked in any way, you will not be able to equalize. In addition, if your sinus or nasal passages are filled or clogged, it will make the air spaces in your head a lot smaller.

Think of our bottle and balloon example again only this time the bottle is half filled with jello. The jello prevents the air from flowing between the balloon and the bottle and therefore the elastic balloon cannot compensate for the negative pressure in the bottle. Not only does the bottle get squeezed but because the jello is already filling up half of the air space in the bottle, the remaining space is compressed rapidly. Can you guess what happens in your head? That's right – it implodes – and believe me you don't want to experience this.

My only experience with this was several years ago when I took my kids to a swimming pool. I had a lingering sinus infection and I thought it might do some good to swim around in a heated indoor pool. I was not thinking about water pressure at all. Innocently, I dove into the pool and only went down about three feet. I immediately came to the surface, screaming in pain. Quite literally, it felt like my head was going to explode when I entered the water. I felt a pain so intense and so sudden. It was a feeling that I will not forget and it was only three feet down. I'm sharing this story so that you can appreciate the seriousness of this. Hopefully it will prevent someone else from going through the same painful experience.

Buoyancy Control

Buoyancy is your ability to either float or sink in the water. Positive buoyancy makes you float toward the surface and negative buoyancy makes you sink to the bottom. Neutral buoyancy is a term used when you are in the water and you are neither sinking nor floating. You just sort of hang in one area of the water column.

Try this experiment if you haven't already. In the deep end of a swimming pool blow out all of the air in your lungs until you have nothing left. Then just lie still and observe what happens. As you might have guessed, you sink or become negatively buoyant. Conversely, if you are in the same situation and you inhale a deep breath and then hold it, what happens? That's right; you float or become positively buoyant.

What you are doing is inflating and deflating your own personal floatation devices – your lungs. So what happens in our experiment when you take a deep breath at the surface and then dive to the bottom of the pool? The air that you have trapped in your lungs will slowly float you up to the surface. See if you can blow out a little bit of that air until you find yourself suspended in the water or neutrally buoyant.

When you get the hang of equalizing properly, you will be able to dive very deep without discomfort. As you start to go deeper you will soon notice that it gets colder and colder the further you go down. To protect yourself from the cold you will need to wear a wetsuit. I will give you a lot of wetsuit information in a later chapter but for now you will need to know a few wetsuit facts.

A wetsuit does an excellent job keeping you warm by enabling your body to heat up a thin layer of water between you and your suit. Wetsuits are made out of many different materials and in a variety of thicknesses depending upon how much warmth you require. The rubber of a wetsuit contains "cells" which are tiny pockets of air within the suit. Tiny pockets of air float. Therefore, your wetsuit floats. If you put on a full body wetsuit and try to dive down underwater it is nearly impossible to get very far below the surface. The diver must compensate for this excess in positive buoyancy by adding some negative buoyancy to his body in the form of lead weights.

The typical weight system consists of a nylon belt with several lead weights attached to the belt. The amount of weight that you need to attach to your belt depends on your size and weight and the size of your wetsuit. For example, if you weigh 140 pounds and you have a 3 mm wetsuit, you will need a lot less weight than someone who weighs 220 pounds and wears a 7mm wetsuit. We will get into the reasons for different wetsuits later but the point that I am trying to make here is that I cannot tell you exactly how much weight you need to balance out your buoyancy. You will have to play with this a bit and vary the weight while diving different depths to see what works best for you.

The interesting part about a wetsuit and the air cells within it is that the same rules of positive and negative pressure apply to the air in the cells as well. When you dive down, the pressure compresses these air cells and as they get smaller, they become less buoyant. So as you go deeper, you wetsuit sinks easier. As you swim back toward the surface, the positive pressure expands these air cells and makes your wetsuit more positively buoyant.

You may be wondering how this affects the amount of weight you need to get you below the surface. The amount of weight will also depend upon how deep you are trying to dive. For example, let's say you are going to a place where you are going to dive 12 feet to get to the bottom. Try first to get to the bottom without any weight. What happens? You won't even get below the surface because your wetsuit acts like a life preserver at the surface with all of those full cells.

Next, add a little weight to your belt. Try about 5 pounds. With this added weight you may be able to get below the surface and struggle to get to the bottom. However, when you get to the bottom and begin to look for fish, your wetsuit still has not compressed very much and keeps you positively buoyant. You float right back up – or struggle to try to stay on the bottom. Either way, you have scared away all of the fish because you look like a clumsy, floundering, human who does not belong there.

You conclude that you must add significantly more weight to your belt in order to easily get to the bottom so let's try adding about 20 more pounds. Now you have 25 pounds of lead strapped to your belt and you jump in the water. Struggling to keep your head above water, you begin to sink like a stone. When you get to the bottom, you have no trouble staying there. However, when it's time to come back to the surface it is an exhausting swim that drains most of your already spent energy. When you get there, you continually struggle to keep you head up and have a miserable time. Conclusion: obviously too much weight.

Back and forth you remove weight and add weight and try again and again. Finally you will find a suitable weight that will enable you to float easily at the surface without having to kick or swim much at all. At the same time this weight will also allow you to submerge easily and help to weigh you down just enough to stay perfectly still on the bottom. When it's time to come up, give a good kick off the bottom. As you start to rise, the positive pressure in your wetsuit should start to take effect and aid your ascent to the surface with minimal effort on your part. That is when you know you have the correct weight for optimal buoyancy control.

A deep swimming pool is the ideal place to work on this. Take all the time you need to make sure that your wetsuit and weight system are in balance before you put it to the test in the ocean.

I mentioned earlier that the amount of weight will also depend on how deep you are planning to dive. Here's where buoyancy control gets a little more complicated. In our previous example, we were diving to a depth of 12 feet. Now let's see what happens when we dive to 30 feet.

You've found your ideal weight for a 12 foot dive to be 18 pounds. At the surface, everything is fine because your suit and weights are balanced for the most part. Dive down and imagine for a minute what is going on around you when you get to the 12 foot mark. You have just become negatively buoyant. Deeper you go and now you are at the 20 foot mark. The cells in your wetsuit are significantly compressed now and have lost most of their floatation. If you had no weight at all you may just be hovering there at 20 feet. But now 18 pounds of lead really starts to take effect. You start dropping like a stone to the bottom again. You make it to 30 feet in a hurry and at the end of your breath you give a good kick to get off the bottom. As you start to swim upward to the 20 foot point, that 18 pounds of lead is weighing heavy on your belt.

You have some choices to make at this point. You could give in to the weight and drop steadily back to 30 feet and remain there for a long, long time. You could kick like mad against the strain of your weights to get past that 12 foot point so that your wetsuit will again help your ascent. Or you can unbuckle your weight belt; drop it to the bottom and swim freely back to the surface where there is air. None of these options is very appealing.

The best thing to do is to know ahead of time how much weight you are going to need for the specific depth you are planning on diving. A couple pounds over or under is not going to make too much difference but getting as close as you can to the ideal weight will make your experience a lot more enjoyable. You want to be able to conserve as much energy as possible. When you use up a lot of energy swimming, you use up a lot of oxygen. In turn this significantly reduces the amount of time you are able to stay underwater.

Safety Matters 2: The Buddy System

The Buddy System is a general term used to emphasize the importance of always diving with a partner. When you are underwater there are so many unpredictable things that could go wrong. If something does go wrong, it's nice to know that someone is there to watch your back. For safety reasons, you should never go diving alone.

While freediving or even while training to freedive it is also important to have a partner close by. Out of all the possible things that could go wrong, the most severe is probably something called the 'shallow water blackout' or SWB. This potentially deadly effect is rare but worth learning about. Personally I have never experienced a SWB but I have read about it on several internet message boards.

When you hold your breath and dive down until you cannot hold your breath any longer, naturally you are going to have to come up to the surface. Many freedivers will try to push this breathhold to its ultimate limit and rise to the surface at the last possible minute. Well, something can happen during those last few seconds when you are completely out of air and unable to take another breath. Your involuntary muscles will try to kick into automatic breathing mode and your voluntary muscles (you can control) will not let them because you are still under water. The result is a system shutdown! You blackout. Now normally, if you were to blackout and you were not underwater, your involuntary muscles will automatically make you breathe - just like when you are sleeping. But since you are underwater and unconscious and you are not a fish, you will not be able to breathe and I think you know how this story ends. Not well, I'm afraid.

Some people who have suffered the SWB claim that they were not even pushing themselves to the breathhold limit when this occurred.

There is some degree of mystery surrounding how and why the SWB actually happens. It has also been suggested that the pressure changes as you go deeper underwater may play some role in the SWB. Because this is such an unpredictable occurrence, having a partner near you at all times while diving is vitally important.

In addition to the SWB there are some other dangers in the underwater environment. A big, big shark is one of them. I think you may be starting to understand how the movie JAWS had such an effect on me. In all seriousness though, sharks are probably pretty low on the danger meter when it comes to diving hazards. You are probably more likely to get speared by your buddy than you are to be attacked by a shark. In that case I would suggest that you choose your buddy wisely in the Buddy System.

Another realistic hazard is getting caught or tangled in something while you are underwater. I have moved under and around lobster trap lines, rock piles, thick kelp, bridge pilings, etc. All of the excellent structure that holds a variety of fish species can also be a potential hazard if you are not careful. A partner nearby can watch your back and alert you to dangers that you may not see. It only takes a split second for something to go wrong underwater for there to be a major tragedy so be careful and be prepared. Anyone who dives should be trained in basic first aid which includes rescue breathing. If you do need to help a partner in distress, it is important that you know what you are doing as well. I am not prepared to go into any first aid lessons here but all divers should have a basic understanding of it. There are internet resources if you want to teach yourself and your local Red Cross offers first aid and CPR trainings on a regular basis.

With everything I've said so far about the Buddy System I have to admit that I am somewhat of a hypocrite. And so are hundreds of spearfishermen. The reason I say this is because spearfishing requires you to be stealthy and quiet. If there is too much movement in the water there is a chance the fish will spook. So, to be a proficient spearfisherman you may not want another person splashing around right near you. We do the next best thing. We go spearfishing with a buddy and although we may go our separate ways when we enter the water, we always look out for each other and stay a reasonable distance away. We use hand signals to let the other person know that everything is alright and we review some emergency signals before each dive. This also minimizes the chance of being speared by your so called buddy.

Chapter 2 – Basic Equipment

When you start reading the next few sections it may seem like the Basic Equipment chapter is anything but basic. True, it can get a little overwhelming but in order to do it right you should at least know about what is available to you. Through experience and trial and error I have made my share of mistakes. When you make mistakes you learn how to approach the next situation better. I will share with you some of my mistakes and successes and hopefully you can use this information to avoid making similar mistakes on your journey.

I don't have all of the right answers and there are new devices being developed all the time to try to improve this sport. I can tell you this – the equipment needed for freediving and spearfishing is quite minimal when compared to SCUBA diving. The following sections will teach you about some equipment preferences that I have. I do a lot of research shopping in order to minimize the expense for my equipment. Some things are expensive and necessary but there are also many things that can be simple and less costly. This will give you a good starting point and from there you can decide what is necessary for you.

Wetsuits

We've already started talking about wetsuits so let's continue on that subject. The wetsuit is one of the very important items to consider when learning about freediving and spearfishing. An ill fitting wetsuit can get you through the day but your comfort is not something you'll want to sacrifice for very long.

For my first couple of years spearfishing, I wore a wetsuit that I thought was right for what I was doing. It was a little difficult to manage at times and after an unfortunate tear in the knee I was inspired to shop for a new one. I did a lot of research and shopping around for my new suit. Since I had a couple of years experience there were now some things that I knew I wanted in a wetsuit - and more importantly some things I knew I didn't want. Sometimes it takes that personal experience in order to gain the knowledge.

When I first started, money was a primary concern. As long as it worked and was within my budget, I was willing to sacrifice some comfort. Later on I came to the realization that comfort in the wetsuit is not exactly just a luxury - it is necessary. If you use a wetsuit that is comfortable, easy to move around in and not too constricting, you will be able to relax a lot more while diving. As I said before, relaxation is the key to conserving energy and oxygen and therefore extending your dive time.

My research brought me to a great online spearfishing forum called www.deeperblue.com. I was able to ask many other spearfishermen, who had a lot more experience than I, and I was steered in the direction of my new suit. There are many, many options out there and after you narrow down your options it may be just a matter of picking one from the many suits available. One that was right for me may not be right for you.

I liked a company called Elios (eliossub.com) who custom designed my wetsuit and shipped it to me from Europe. Sounds extreme doesn't it? Well to be quite honest with you, it was less expensive than many of the suits that were available at local dive shops or even online dive shops. I had to pay in Euros but I simply used my credit card and the dollar conversion was made for me. Looking back, I think I spent about $250 for the whole thing which included pants, long sleeve top with a hood, gloves, and booties.

What I liked about this suit was the price, the fit and the stretch. There were a variety of materials to choose from. One thing in particular that I hated about my first suit was that it felt so tight. It was sized right for me but it was not very forgiving and I felt like I was in a full body cast when I had it on. With my new suit I found a material called hyperstretch which is fantastic. Once it was on it felt very comfortable and allowed me to breathe freely without much effort or constriction from the material. This, I found, was the most important aspect in selecting a great spearfishing wetsuit.

Let me also mention for a moment the material that the wetsuit is made from. The typical wetsuit used by scuba divers and surfers is made with wetsuit rubber on the inside and some type of nylon exterior. The purpose is for the nylon to be protective and somewhat durable and resistant to tearing. The inside rubber is the insulator. It fits so tightly to your skin that it practically acts like another skin. When you dive in, water enters the wetsuit and a thin layer of water remains between your skin and the rubber. The heat from your body warms the water and it is trapped there by the rubber. Throughout your dive new water circulates through but the layer of water is so thin that it is easily heated by your body and conserved by the suit.

As the water gets colder, you can protect yourself with a thicker wetsuit. For my area a 5mm wetsuit is typical to combat water temperatures in the 60-70 degree range. The only problem is that when your wetsuit gets thicker, it also gets tighter and more constricting. The hyperstretch material in my new suit seems to have worked out that problem. I still have the 5mm thickness for warmth but the material is so stretchy and soft that I do not feel constricted.

With the advantages in the hyperstretch also come some compromises. My suit is made with a super-elastic rubber neoprene on the outside and an elastic nylon interior. Having the super-elastic on the outside makes this suit extremely fragile. Therefore, I have to be extra careful when I am near rock piles, mussel beds, barnacles, or any other structures. Slight tears in this suit's surface can compromise its ability to stretch as well as its insulating capacity.

Another problem that I always had with my previous suit was being able to get it on and take it off. I felt like I was an escape artist trying to get in and out of a straight jacket. I can remember getting to my dive location and using up so much energy just getting my suit on that I had to wait so long before I was able to relax enough to dive. Very frustrating. Then I started making a soapy water concoction that I would fill in a gallon jug and bring it with me. Before getting into my suit I would pour this slurry into the arms and legs of my suit and it would make the rubber really slippery. I slid right in. Taking the wetsuit off was an equally daunting task. Often, the rubber would stick to my skin after being in it for a while. I had to be careful not to tear the suit just taking it off.

The elastic nylon on the inside of my new suit combined with the super-elastic exterior made this process a lot easier. It was almost as simple as putting on a sweatshirt. Almost. I didn't have to remember my soapy water slurry any longer. I didn't notice much, if any, compromise in insulation due to the rubber being on the outside. I seemed to stay as warm as my previous suit had kept me.

Another advantage to my new suit was the custom fit. It wasn't just a stock wetsuit off the shelf with sizes L, XL, etc. The Elios company was extremely thorough in properly sizing my suit to my body. It was all done online with a measurement guide. I measured every dimension of my body and filled in the guide. The result was a form fitting three dimensional custom suit. The stock wetsuits are flat for the most part and do not conform to the way that the arms and body tend to flex. Again, all of these factors add to the comfort and fit for a reason – to make you more relaxed and to make you breathe as freely as possible while diving.

I think that the only thing I sacrificed in my suit was its durability. I recently checked back to the Elios website and noticed that they now have the same type of suit that I purchased but in addition they offer it with a new mesh skin. It is an improvement to the super-elastic neoprene that is more resistant to cuts and abrasions. Sounds like something I'd be interested in the next time I'm in the market.

All in all, the price was right and the comfort and fit were just what I was looking for. Other suits out there are in the price range of $300-$400 or more and don't offer the custom sizing. It did take a little while longer to have it made and shipped to me in the US but I started the process in the winter so that it was sure to be ready when the warmer weather arrived.

I mentioned the components of my wetsuit earlier – pants, hood, gloves, booties, etc. I think it's worth mentioning the reasons for these specific parts. I've seen wetsuits come in a variety of styles. There are one-piece, two-piece, shorties, farmer johns, etc. Personally I prefer a two-piece style. I started with a one-piece and found it to be constricting. I also like the flexibility of being able to take the top off to cool down between dives on occasion.

Shorties are primarily for warmer temperatures. I had no use for this type in Rhode Island but in Florida I'm sure they're quite popular. Farmer Johns are a style where the pant bottoms are held up by a type of suspender and a sleeved top is worn over your torso. This is similar to the two-piece variety. The two-piece that I have has a neoprene strap on the top portion that goes under your crotch and attaches on the other side. If I did have one complaint about this style it's the crotch strap.

Another option is to get a hooded or non-hooded top. Again this is a personal preference. In colder water I don't even think this is an option – it's a must. If you plan on owning just one suit for now the hooded option is probably best. The benefits of a hood are: keeps your head warm, prevents direct flow of water into your ears, and protects your head (from big sharks of course). Seriously though, there are times when you swim through masses of seaweed, tiny crab hatches, worms and other small animals and most notably through jellyfish. Being completely covered in neoprene gives me the added security I need to swim through any of that stuff without a care. I've gone a few times without the hood and found myself a bit paranoid.

In addition to the hood you may also consider the option of using gloves and dive booties. We'll discuss fins in more detail later and to some degree this will dictate the type of footwear you will use. I prefer a neoprene sock that is the same thickness as my wetsuit. Sometimes I need thicker booties if the water is really cold because I had a frostbite experience while skiing when I was younger. Ever since, I found that my feet and toes are particularly susceptible to the cold.

Gloves are important because they enable you to comfortably grab onto a variety of things underwater without the fear of damaging your hands and fingers. When you are in the water for long periods of time, your fingers and hands get a bit soft. It is very easy to get cuts and abrasions if you're not careful. Your extremities like fingers and toes are more easily chilled in cold water so do not underestimate the importance here. I have used a variety of gloves and have found that the combination of flexibility and warmth works the best. Some stock gloves are flat and do not conform to the bends in your hands and fingers. Some gloves that provide significant warmth by being thicker are a bit constricting and don't offer much in the way of comfort.

When you spearfish you need your hands for a variety of fine motor skills. You need to be able to comfortably hold your speargun and have good feeling on the trigger. After taking a shot you will need to reload your speargun underwater and this means being able to manipulate the cord that attaches your spear to your speargun. Your gloves must be thin enough to feel all of the parts of the speargun in the reload process. Your gloves also provide thickness needed to get a good grip on the power bands that load the speargun. This takes some strength and leverage and having a good grip helps tremendously.

When you shoot a fish you will need to subdue it fairly quickly. Fish are slippery, slimy, scaled, spiked and toothy all at once. This is the moment you will appreciate your gloves most of all. A good grip on the fish's gills will most certainly restrain it well and a good pair of gloves will keep your sensitive hands out of harm's way.

As you can see, gloves need to be multifunctional. Thick enough that they protect and warm your hands, but thin enough that they provide the feeling and dexterity you need. My advice is to try on a variety of gloves if they are available. If not, you may have to purchase gloves that are thin and flexible and another pair that are thick and protective. Get a feel for both of them to see what you prefer. I know some people who do both. On their shooting hand they have a thin glove and on their fish grappling hand they have a thicker glove. Not a bad idea. More about gloves later when we talk about grabbing lobsters.

To summarize this section about wetsuits I must say that comfort is the key and if you try to skimp on comfort because of cost you will pay for it in the end. Sometimes, however, it takes a bit of trial and error and personal experience to realize this fact. Hopefully the information that I provided for you here will give you a starting point and maybe you can use some of my experiences to weed through many of the varieties of wetsuits out there. A super-elastic material will enable you to breathe easy and move comfortably. The other options may depend a lot on the area you live or the locations you plan to dive. The thicker your wetsuit, the more positively buoyant it will be so the next subject to discuss is your weight system.

Weight Systems

As you might imagine, there are a variety of weight systems available. What a surprise - more choices and more questions. Let's start with the most basic and then go from there. As you add options, you will add expense but you will also add comfort so once again you are going to have to balance comfort with cost.

The most basic weight system is a nylon weight belt strung with block lead weights. There is a quick release buckle (a requirement with all the weight systems) which will enable you to quickly drop your weights in an emergency. The benefit of this system is the cost. The drawback is that the nylon does not have any stretch to it. When you freedive with a wetsuit the compression from the pressure difference causes you to get a little skinnier as you submerge. As you ascend you will expand a bit. The nylon belt does not self adjust to compensate for this change. Once it is buckled it is a fixed length and it tends to slide up and down your body a bit when you change your body position. This is where a rubber belt is helpful.

A rubber belt will stretch just enough to stay put when you go up and down in the water. In addition to its flexibility it is made out of rubber which sticks very well against a neoprene wetsuit. The point I'm trying to make here is that you don't want your weights sliding all over the place when you dive. Shifting weight will throw you off a bit and again comfort will be compromised. When shopping for a rubber weight belt it is sometimes referred to as a Marseillaise belt. I'm not sure what that means but I had a hard time finding one once because I didn't know what to search for. Now you know. They're a little more expensive than the nylon belts but less expensive than some of the other systems that I will soon describe. Therefore, the Marseillaise belt is an excellent starting belt – easy to use and easy to get used to.

The two belts that I described thus far are waist belts. They concentrate their weight directly over your waist – in the middle of your body. Sometimes this can be a disadvantage. When I approach the sea bottom and start looking for fish I sometimes notice my legs starting to float upward. This can be annoying and break my concentration on my breathhold. Some people find that the solution here is to add a pound or so of weight to each leg in the form of ankle weights. By placing some weight on each ankle you are more evenly distributing the weight across your body and different body parts don't float around unnecessarily. Personally, I don't use ankle weights but I can see the benefit. The problem with ankle weights is that they cannot be easily released in an emergency and I imagine that they are cumbersome while swimming at the surface.

I do like the idea of evenly distributing the weight. Another weight system option that accomplishes this is the harness. A weight harness is like a vest that you can buckle and the straps enable your shoulders to support the bulk of the weight. This is particularly helpful when you are out of the water. Toting around 16-20 pounds of lead can get uncomfortable very quickly strapped around your waist. But, when your shoulders and back help with the lifting, it becomes a lot easier. There are several types of weight harnesses available. They uniquely distribute weight by having pockets, attachments and sometimes weight plates in a back pouch. In each design they do their best to incorporate some type of quick release system for emergency situations. Some do a better job than others and some are better suited for SCUBA diving than freediving.

When using pockets to contain the weight it is common to use something called soft weights rather than lead blocks. Soft weights are specifically portioned lead shot weights (tiny balls of lead) in a water proof, mesh bag. It's like a heavy bean bag. The benefit to using soft weights in a pocket is that you can add or remove weight bags very quickly and easily to adjust your overall weight. This is particularly helpful when you are diving in an area that has a variety of depths. When you enter a very shallow area you will need to add weight in order to get down and stay down. It is more cumbersome to add block weights to a waist belt than to slip a bag of soft weights into a pocket.

The downside to some harnesses is that they are made out of nylon and don't have that nice rubber on rubber, no slip contact. I have seen some recently on the market that are made from neoprene. This would be advantageous for the same reasons that the rubber belt is better than the nylon belt. Another disadvantage to nylon and soft weights is that they do not dry as quickly as block weights and rubber belts. This can be inconvenient when you are cleaning and drying your equipment between trips.

The harnesses are more expensive than the belts. I've seen them for as much as $200 for the harness and then weights can cost another $50 or so. For the beginner I would again recommend the Marseillaise or rubber type waist belt. When you gain some experience and don't mind the extra expense you may want to give the harness a try. I lost my rubber belt in a kayak flipping mishap and decided to buy a weight harness from a local dive shop. After using it a few times I'm not completely convinced that it is significantly better than my old system. It's a lot more comfortable walking around out of the water but that's not really what we're concerned about here. A little more time will tell if this is going to be the right weight system for me.

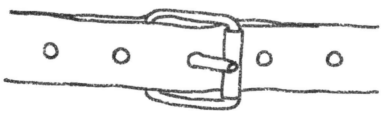

Masks

A well fitting mask is sometimes difficult to find. The shape of your face is unique and not every mask will fit. For such an important piece of equipment, I would recommend that you put the time in and go directly to the dive shops to try some masks on your face. You can tell almost immediately if a mask is not right for you. When you press it to your face and slightly breathe in to create suction, if there are any uncomfortable pinches or air leaks or other defects, you'll know right away. That's where a dive shop comes in handy. With a wide variety of choices and shapes and sizes you will most likely find one that works for you.

Avoid the pre-packaged mask-snorkel-fin combo packs! The price may be attractive now but you will pay the price for your laziness when you start to dive. Remember my friends Greg and Pete? They had a very tight budget and were willing to sacrifice some comforts in order to get into the water as quickly as possible. They found most of the equipment that they needed to get started at a local K-Mart and for under $100 they had a mask, snorkel, fins and wetsuit. I don't mean to knock K-Mart – they provide an excellent service by offering such a wide variety of items – but for this purpose, Greg and Pete would learn their first lesson. Sacrificing their comfort by not investing in the proper equipment would prove to be a problem.

I invited Greg and Pete out on my boat to try spearfishing with them for the first time. I verbally ran through all of the necessary equipment and it seemed as though they were minimally prepared. They were proud of their recent purchases and they were both very excited to get started. When we arrived at our dive location and started to put on our gear, the first thing I noticed was Greg's mask. It had an oval shaped, glass face that enclosed his eyes as well as his nose. I knew at the time that this would make it impossible for him to equalize properly because he could not pinch his nose closed. I knew that this would prevent him from going any deeper than about

10 feet without feeling the intense squeeze from the water pressure. Instead of criticizing Greg's purchase, I decided to just let him figure some of these things out for himself. There was no point in making an issue out of it. We were already out there and we weren't going to come in because of the mask.

After his first few attempts at diving down deep he began to feel the pressure. I briefly warned him not to try to exceed the depth at which he started to get uncomfortable. We were seeing some fish and he was pushing himself to get to the depth he needed to go. After a short while he felt too uncomfortable to continue – A perfect time for the first of many lessons to be taught to Greg.

Greg was a big guy and could hold a breath for a long time. He was mostly frustrated because he could not figure out why his ears hurt so much when he tried to dive to where the fish were. And more specifically, how was I able to do this without feeling the pain. I told Greg what I had learned at the SCUBA class about water pressure and equalizing. I showed him my mask more closely and what was not apparent to him before became very clear now. The soft rubber around my nose was not just there to look cool but was there for a reason. After taking some time to regroup and to talk about the science, I let Greg try on my mask and take some dives to practice what he had just learned about equalizing.

Greg noticed an immediate difference. In the case of equalizing, a little knowledge can go a long way. The first comfort hurdle that Greg had to get past was the fact that his mask would definitely not work for the type of diving we were doing. It was a snorkeling mask – not a freediving mask. At the surface and down to about 5 feet it was perfectly fine. It had a large glass face which made it easy to see a lot. It was inexpensive. Good for some things, but not for our purpose. It was clear to Greg at this point that he would have to make a trip to the dive shop and invest some more money in a better quality dive mask.

A great mask doesn't have to be too expensive. If you do your homework and shop around you should be able to find a perfectly acceptable freediving mask for about $30-40. The higher end masks sell for around $100-150. For the additional price you may get specially tinted lenses or a more comfortable, form fitting skirt. The skirt is that part of the mask that surrounds your face and makes a water tight seal. Again, you have to weigh the benefits of comfort and cost and decide what is right based on your situation.

Once you know the general type of mask that works for you and fits your face right, you can then spend some time looking online or reading spearfishing forums about the types of masks specifically designed for either freediving or more specifically spearfishing. As a beginner, don't get too caught up in the variety out there. Get a reasonably priced mask that fits and use it. You will most likely figure out, just as Greg did, the things you like about your mask and the things that you don't like. When it comes time to re-invest in upgraded equipment you will have your own experiences to fall back on.

I lost a $100 mask one day (in that kayak flipping incident) and it forced me to go see what else was out there. While shopping online I stumbled upon a unique mask design and I gave it a try. It looks like a typical dive mask but attached to the strap on both sides are two rubber cups that fit over your ears – almost like earmuffs. In addition, there is a small air tube that connects each ear cup to the main chamber of the mask that is over your face and nose. The air that is in your mask is essentially connected to the air surrounding your ears. Can you guess why this might be helpful? Think about the air pressure situation when you make a deep dive.

The theory behind a mask like this was to connect your air spaces from the outside of your ears to your nose. This would allow you to release a little air out of your nose thereby providing air to your external ear spaces. The idea was to assist in equalizing without having to hold your nose and push that negative pressure out. I am purposely using terms like "theory" and "idea" because my actual experiences with this mask were quite different.

I bought this mask because it was relatively inexpensive (around $40) and I really liked the idea of not having to hold my nose to equalize. However, in all fairness to the mask, I did not use it in the exact way that it was intended and as a result I found myself needing to equalize in the traditional way anyway. Confused yet? Let me explain. Remember my discussion about the wetsuit hood? Well, the wetsuit hood covers over your ears. And since I am a firm believer of the wetsuit hood it didn't do me much good to cover over my already covered ears with mask earmuffs. This external air space was already blocked and therefore the earmuff to nose air connection was rendered useless.

I did a little experimenting with this mask in a swimming pool without my wetsuit and it did seem to work in the way it was designed. The true test would have been in a much deeper environment but since I live in New Jersey and not the Virgin Islands, I wasn't willing to give the mask a fair deep water test. Would I recommend it for people living in warmer water areas? Sure. Give it a try. That's the cool thing about this sport – there are lots of gizmos that people are continually developing in order to improve the experience. Keep trying new things until you figure out what equipment is right for you.

After rejecting the ear muff mask I started doing some research again to locate the best mask for my purpose. I was searching for a small mask with very little air space between your face and the glass. I also wanted the skirt to be very soft and comfortable and able to make and keep an airtight seal. Ideally I wanted the glass to curve a bit around my face so that I would have some peripheral vision. I was also considering a glass with some tint to it. I have seen masks with mirror lenses, some with a blue or yellow tint to them and others that are dark or polarizing like sunglasses. If you wear glasses you can even have a prescription glass lens made for your dive mask. The more you customize a mask, the higher the price tag – as you can imagine.

Having a small mask with little air space was a big priority for me. Can you imagine why? There's that air space issue creeping up again. Picture yourself holding your breath and diving down deep and think about only the air space between your face and your mask. The skirt has sealed up the edges so no water or air can get in and as you dive down the air space starts to compress. Instinctively when you hold your breath you close off the passage from your lungs to your nose by using the muscles in your throat and soft palate. When you go down around 15 to 20 feet the effects of the compression are not very noticeable on your face. However, when you start going beyond that 20 foot mark you start to really feel a "sucking" effect as the mask air space compresses. This really sucks. Slowly, as you go deeper and deeper your eyeballs start to get literally pulled out of your head! This is not a very good feeling. You need to fix this – and quickly! Go back up? No way man – there are fish down there to shoot. Simple fix – relax those muscles in the back of your throat and let a little bit of air out from your lungs and out your nose. Whoa – what a relief. Your eyeballs settle back down into their sockets. Well done, crisis averted. Is there a point to all this? Yes, just give me a second to explain.

When you freedive, every bit of air is precious. Any air that you let out of your lungs equals seconds of time that you will lose underwater. Air = Time. The goal is to preserve as much of that air as possible and that means – do not blow air out of your nose unless you absolutely have to. And when you have to, blow out as little as possible to prevent your eyes from being sucked out of your head. So if you have a small air space in your mask you will only need to replace that compressed air with a very little bit of air from your lungs in order to equalize your face.

The best way to buy a mask is to go to a shop with a large variety and try them on. Without strapping the mask around your head, put the mask up to your face and suck in slightly with your nose. You should be able to hold the mask on your face with little effort. The skirt should seal well and cause a suction that prevents it from falling off. The skirt should also be soft and comfortable and under a constant pressure it shouldn't jab you anywhere. Pay close attention to this. Masks are made in many different shapes and sizes to accommodate all the faces available so find one that fits your face comfortably and you will be very glad you put the time in. Few things are worse to a spearfisherman than having part of the mask gauging you under your nose all day long. Remember the formula for success:

Comfort = Less Stress = More Air = More Time = More Fish = More Fun

Do not sacrifice your comfort if you can help it.

Tinted glass lenses are available and may have their place in certain diving situations. I have heard that some species of fish may tune in to your eyes and get the feeling they are being watched. This can cause them to spook more easily. I'm not sure how much truth there is to this but some of these masks do look pretty cool. This can add a bit to your cost so you really have to decide if you think it is worth it.

Whichever mask you decide on, it is important to treat the glass properly so that it stays clear and does not fog when you are diving. A foggy mask means more stress and I think you know what that eventually means (see previous equation). If your newly purchased mask has not been chemically treated to resist fogging, there are some things you may be able to do to get it dive ready. One trick I know is to take some toothpaste and a soft bristle toothbrush and thoroughly scrub the lens on both sides for a few minutes. Then wash it off. I wish I knew the idea behind this but I don't. All I know is that it is a way to remove some of the factory chemicals that went into the mask making process and this enables you to keep your mask from fogging.

Additionally, each time you dive you will have to coat the inside of your mask with some type of surfactant that helps the mask resist fogging. Without getting into many different products available for this purpose, good old fashioned saliva will work just fine. Shoot a nice wad of spit into your mask and rub it all around on the inside just before you put it on for your first dive of the day. Rinse it out with some water and you are good to go. I do carry with me one product that is worth mentioning. It is a little bottle that I keep right in my mask case and it is appropriately named, "Spit." I don't think that the people who invented this product are actually spitting into bottles and selling them for $5. But it is good stuff and seems to last all day long. It is a little thicker than your home grown variety of spit and seems to stick better to the glass. There are many other products available for this purpose but if you find yourself out on the water without any, feel comfortable in the fact that your body will make some up for you in a pinch.

Snorkels

Remember my reference earlier about Less Stress = More Air? Well a good snorkel can make the difference between a highly stressful surface interval and a very relaxed one. The surface interval is the time spent between dives that will allow you to catch your breath and thoroughly oxygenate your body. During this time you should be face down, relaxing on the surface of the water and breathing in and out of your snorkel. Your wetsuit and weights have you in a position that you shouldn't have to struggle at all to stay perfectly flat and perfectly still. This is your time to take it all in. Practice your yoga or meditation and enjoy just being out there in the wonderful blue ocean just floating around. DO NOT THINK OF SHARKS at any point during your surface interval! Remember this sentence – and then put it out of your head for good. This is a time for enjoyment and reflecting on life and all of its little pleasures. You're going to be up here floating around for most of your freediving/spearfishing day. Find your happy place. Your goal is to get your heart rate down, relax and breathe. The oxygen needs to be replenished in your lungs, blood, muscles and brain. All you have to do is breathe. And don't think of sharks! Really – don't do it. You will enjoy your experience much more if you can follow that one simple rule.

Ok, so you're breathing at the surface feeling really good about your day and your accomplishments and all the fish you are about to catch. One of the worst things that can happen to you at this point is to suck in a bunch of sea water instead of air. Well, I wrote that last sentence and after reading it back silently to myself my imagination got the best of me. I suppose a boat could go speeding by and grind you up in the propellers – and there are always those sharks. But since we are talking about snorkels here, let's stick to the topic. Your snorkel is there to get you the most air possible while keeping the water out. As you might have already guessed there are many different snorkel designs out there and it is your job to weed through them to find out which one is the best for you.

The hunt for the perfect snorkel has been quite a journey for me. A task, I must admit, that is still an ongoing adventure. I am always open to trying out new things so my first couple snorkels were pretty interesting. My primary goal when I started snorkeling was to prevent water from getting into my breath. I can't tell you how annoying this can be. You just have to experience it for yourself but it is extremely stressful especially when you are trying to relax. One breath of water can ruin your whole rhythm. Frustrating.

My first snorkel had this contraption attached to the end of the snorkel tube that was designed to keep water out. If this snorkel went under water, a little float valve would close off the end and block out the water. The only trouble was that it also blocked off the air. The second most frustrating thing about a snorkel is getting no air when you need it. I managed with this snorkel for a long time. I was willing to learn how to get around the no air problem as long as the snorkel stayed dry. It also had a one way valve near the mouthpiece that enabled me to blow out any water that managed to get in. This snorkel was somewhat expensive (around $45) and until the kayak flipping incident I was content to continue using this as my primary snorkel. After the incident, and the loss of much of my equipment, I decided to rethink some of my snorkel choices and consider other options.

Two things I disliked about that snorkel were the previously mentioned air blocking as well as the fact that it rattled around a bit underwater. That air/water valve float would continually move and make a little clinking plastic sound while I was trying to hunt fish and stay as quiet as possible. It was time to make some changes. I decided that when it comes to a snorkel, simpler is better.

Now that I have become much more experienced on the surface of the water I do not have as much need for a device with a valve that keeps the water out. I simply change the angle of my head and prevent the end of the snorkel from getting submerged. What I really needed was a snorkel that allowed me to get the biggest breath of stress free, oxygenated air possible. This involved a very wide tube that was not restricted by any valves or gizmos. Big breath in, big breath out. Simple. Sure, I knew a little water would get in from time to time but having a wide tube also gives you the ability to blow that water out very easily. The other advantage of this snorkel was that it had no moving parts. Nothing to clank around underwater and nothing to accidentally block off the air flow when you need it.

The simple snorkel also has the advantage of having a simple price tag. I got mine for $14 and if I am in a situation where my misfortune leaves me looking for a new snorkel again, I will not fret at the notion of getting another simple one.

Fins

It is very easy to identify someone who is freediving by the length of their fins. It is unmistakable. This is the area where the Kmart special mask, snorkel, fin combo will just not do. Fins are an item that you will most likely want to invest a little more money in to get a set best suited for spearfishing. In general, longer is better. Your investment in a high quality set of long fins will be rewarded by the fact that they will last a very long time. I am still diving with the first set of fins that I started with on my spearfishing adventure and have never even considered another set. That's the only piece of equipment that I can say that about. The cost for a good set of fins will run between $100 and $200.

Now I'm not saying that you can't get started with an out of the box set of typical snorkeling fins. If your budget is the primary concern then by all means get the Kmart special to start. One way to learn this game is to experience it all for yourself and then make changes as you progress. For $30 or less you may be able to equip yourself with a box set just to get into the water. Perfectly acceptable. But when you're ready to start making upgrades, a good set of fins will make your life underwater a whole lot easier.

Remember the Low Stress equation right? Well, when it comes to swimming around in the ocean all day your leg muscles are going to be your workhorse. Your hands are going to be preoccupied with other things and you will be kicking to propel yourself everywhere you go. With shorter fins your legs will have to kick a lot more to get from place to place and this translates into using a lot more energy. When you use more energy than necessary, your leg muscles require a lot more oxygenated blood to work properly. And guess what folks – the oxygen has to come from somewhere. When you are underwater, the only oxygen available to you is what you have taken in and held in your lungs on your breath. So if we continue on this train of thought, it should be obvious now that when you expend more energy than necessary, you will run out of oxygen quicker and shorten your breath.

With longer fins you will have to kick less to get from place to place and this translates to using less energy. Conserving energy is one of the primary goals of a spearfisherman. Anything that allows you to comfortably stay underwater longer will greatly increase your chances of success.

In addition to expending less energy, long fins are faster. With each kick from a long fin you will propel significantly further than if you were using short fins. It's just simply a more efficient way to travel through the water. On land – a different story all together. If you want to be proficient at walking with fins on land then most definitely the shorter fin is the way to go. Without a doubt, the long fins are close to impossible to navigate when out of the water. So remember to put them on last – right before you are about to get wet. And take them off first – right before you get out of the water. After all, that's why fish don't have legs.

How long is long enough? Honestly, some people really get carried away here. The true freediver can often be seen with fins almost as long as their body. This is a little overkill if you ask me. Another thing to consider is the fact that you will be on the bottom until you are finished with your breath. To get back to air you will stand up and give a good kick or jump up off the bottom. If your fins are unusually long then this may not be an easy task.

A good spearfishing fin should be about 30-36 inches long. It should be durable, yet flexible and have a molded foot that is comfortable when wearing neoprene booties. If the rubber is too stiff around your foot you will get cramps while kicking. Cramps = Stress. The foot insert does have to be snug so that it doesn't kick off, but not so snug that it cramps your foot. It's a good idea to try fins on in the store before you buy but there is no substitute for an on the water field test. Some dive shops will rent freedive fins so that you can try them before you buy. This makes the best sense when you are considering a significant financial investment.

The new diver is going to experience foot cramping no matter how great the fins fit. You have to understand that when you get into the water for the first time you will be using muscles that you have never used before. It is only natural that your body will have to make some adjustments to this new environment. It takes a long time to get used to wearing fins. Especially long fins because even though they are much more efficient, they do have more water resistance and that means it will take a little more effort to use them. A swimming pool is the best place to practice getting used to new fins. Work out all of the bugs before you use them for spearfishing.

Speargun

There are so many things to say about the speargun that it could be a subject covered in an entire book by itself. For our purposes I am going to try to stick with the basics and focus on one type of gun that is suitable for a very wide variety of hunting situations.

I hunt in the ocean off the Northeast coast of North America and the fish that I target can be anything from a two pound flounder to a fifty pound striped bass on any given dive. I need to have enough power and distance to shoot a big fish but I also have to be smart when approaching a fish in rocky cover with a fully powered up gun. If you shoot into rocks you risk bending a spear, damaging your gun or potentially injuring yourself. The gun that I chose for its versatility in my environment is a medium sized, mid handle, wooden speargun called a Riffe. Riffe is actually the brand or trademark name for the company that develops this type of speargun as well as many other products dedicated to the sport of spearfishing. I have no affiliation with this company other than to say I own one of their guns which, from this point forward will be referred to as my Riffe. There are many other brands of similar style guns but because I am not personally familiar with any of them I will be focusing this next section on the details and components of my Riffe.

The way a speargun works is pretty simple. It's basically a cross between a sling shot and a crossbow. A long metal spear or shaft fits into a groove along the top of the gun. The gun is loaded by stretching a thick elastic band that is fixed to the front of the gun and attaching it to the shaft near the back of the gun. There is a trigger mechanism which, when fired, releases the shaft and the stretch from the elastic band propels the spear forward toward the target. There is typically a shooting line attached to the shaft so the spear can be retrieved after being fired.

Spearguns are offered in a wide variety of sizes depending on your hunting situation. Mine is a midsize which is very versatile. It is about three feet long. When hunting in deep blue offshore waters for very large fish, I typically see very long spearguns being used. The longer guns will give you the ability to shoot targets further away as they are more powerful. The tradeoff is that the longer the gun, the less maneuverable it is in the water. They are also more difficult to load and are more expensive. They certainly have their place and are quite necessary if you plan to hunt pelagic fish like tuna or wahoo but the longer guns are designed for the more experienced spearfisherman and are slightly beyond the scope of this book.

The other extreme is the shorter, pistol style speargun. Designed basically the same way, the short guns can be very useful to the beginner. Obviously, the shorter the gun, the less power you will be able to generate so these guns are not designed for hunting big fish. I had the opportunity once to hunt with friends in some freshwater lakes located within the dense jungle of Belize. The locals used these little spearguns because the fish they were after were not that large and while walking through the jungle it was much easier to carry a very small gun. They maneuver very well, can be loaded quite easily and are less expensive.

For the beginner, this may be a good first gun to purchase in order to become more familiar with the sport. As soon as you come across a fish that seems too big for your gun, it will be time to upgrade. I have not come across that fish yet in my experiences so the midsize gun is still perfect for me in the environment that I typically hunt.

My Riffe is made out of teak. Teak is a very popular wood in the marine industry and can be found on most boats that have wooden parts due to its sturdiness and ability to last a long time in a wet environment. Another benefit of a gun made out of teak is the fact that it floats at the surface but remains pretty much neutrally buoyant when it is underwater. Having neutral buoyancy implies that it does not sink or float while in the water and as a result it makes the gun very easy to swim around with while spearfishing.

Spearguns can also be made out of metal. Lightweight aluminum is a popular choice and metal spearguns can be made virtually identical in size and weight to the wooden variety. I strongly considered a metal Riffe for my speargun purchase because they are slightly less expensive for basically the same gun. The one factor that weighed most heavily with me in making my decision was the fact that a metal gun makes more noise underwater than a wood gun. Attached to the gun are some moving parts like the spear, the shooting line and some metal swivels that attach the parts together. In all fairness, I didn't even try the metal gun but I could picture in my mind all of these little metal parts clinking and clacking together while I was trying to be as quiet and stealthy as possible. So I went with the wood.

The wooden guns are not perfect. They do require some regular maintenance. For the most part it is a good idea to keep your teak well oiled especially if it is sitting out in the sun all day and being dunked into salt water. Every so often I will take a rag dipped in teak oil and rub down the wooden components of my gun. In seconds it looks brand new again. This treatment will also help the gun resist cracking and chipping due to drying out. After many years, this is the only maintenance that I have had to do to my Riffe in order to keep it in great condition.

The spear itself is made out of high strength stainless steel which prevents rust and is very resistant to bending or deformation. It has a barb or flopper on one end close to the point and this prevents the spear from sliding out of the fish once it has been shot. Toward the rear of the spear there are grooves or fins that hold the elastic bands in place once loaded. Additionally, the spear has a long cord attached to the back end which keeps the spear tethered to the gun at all times.

The shooting cord that I use is made from heavy duty monofilament line. This line is about 500 pound test and can be found in tackle stores that are equipped for big game fish rigging. The monofilament has a bit of stretch to it which helps prevent snapping after being shot multiple times. I have not had to change my shooting line for years at a time and have never had one break while spearfishing. That being said, it is very important to never shoot your speargun out of the water for any reason whatsoever. The density of the water controls your gun a bit and absorbs much of the power. If shot out of the water the spearshaft could potentially reach the end limit of the cord and then spring like a rubber band right back at you. There is also the possibility of it snapping the cord and losing the entire shaft. Either way, it is a very dangerous thing to shoot your speargun out of the water so practice good safety and be smart.

The length of this cord will ultimately determine how far you are able to shoot your spear. Obviously, having a longer cord will enable you to shoot fish that are further away but as the distance to your prey increases it becomes more difficult to make a precise shot. There is also a bit of distortion underwater when you look at objects through a mask that are far away from you. The bottom line is, the closer you are to the fish, the better chance you will have to be successful. You will not get a second chance so when you take a shot, make sure it is a good one. Having a super sharp spear will also increase your success rate - especially when shooting at greater distances.

When your spear is sharp it can penetrate almost any area on a fish that it hits. When the point is dull it can either deflect off the fish or possibly blast a larger than expected hole through the back of the fish. Neither of these situations is good so make sure you have a very sharp spear before you go out. I have a grinder wheel in my garage that I use to hone a nice sharp point on the end of my spear. I also keep a metal hand file on my boat so that I can manually file a point in case it gets dull while I am out on a trip. Occasionally I will shoot a fish that is close to structure or rocks and if the sharpened point hits directly on a rock it will damage that point. It's also not a bad idea to take a spare spearshaft along with you in case a spear gets bent out of alignment. Being a little over-prepared is a good thing and it can sometimes save an entire day.

The power of your gun can also be tweaked a bit depending on the hunting situation. For example, if I know I am targeting bottom fish like fluke or structure oriented fish like blackfish, I also know that I may be shooting directly into rocks or whatever is on the bottom underneath that fish. In a case like that, I may not want my gun to be loaded to full power because a direct hit would most assuredly dent my sharp point and possibly bend my shaft. In order to power down I can adjust the number of elastic bands I attach to my spearshaft while loading.

The elastic bands, appropriately called power bands, come in a wide variety of lengths and thicknesses. My Riffe can hold up to three power bands and they are fixed to the front of the gun. Most of the time I am loading all three bands for maximum power and I am being mindful of the structure that I am shooting into. Different styles of spearguns are capable of holding more or less numbers of power bands as well as different thicknesses. The thicker bands will offer more power but will also be more difficult to load.

Additionally, if you get longer or thinner bands they will be easier to load but offer less power. As you may have noticed, it is a bit of a balancing act to find the right number and size bands that are best for your particular situation. This comes from experience and trial and error. Power bands are also a piece of equipment that can and will break while on the water so the smart hunter will have some spare bands on board at all times.

Power bands are fairly easy to make on your own. I recommend to first buy pre-made bands but once you determine the right length and thickness for your gun, you should learn how to make and repair your own bands. Bands will need to be replaced about every other season (depending on how much use they get) so it makes good financial sense to know how to do it. When you get the components to make bands on your own each band will cost a fraction of what the pre-made bands cost but more importantly you will learn how to fix a broken band problem while out on the water. I have had bands break on me while spearfishing and without adequate spare bands or the ability to repair broken bands; a great day can quickly turn into a bad one.

Some spearguns are equipped with a reel mounted to the base of the gun. Similar to a fishing reel, this is spooled with extra line so that a big fish can be reeled in after it has been shot. My Riffe does not have a reel and personally I have never had the need for one. A reel might come in handy for other species of fish like tuna, amberjack or wahoo that tend to really take off after being shot. For the most part, I live in an area where I am not going to have an opportunity to shoot fish like that so a reel is not part of my arsenal. I thought it would be worth mentioning though – for anyone hunting in areas where the species of fish might warrant a reel. Even if you have a gun that doesn't come with a reel, there are conversion kits that will enable you to buy a reel separately and attach it to your gun when needed.

Floatlines

If your speargun, like mine, does not have a reel attached to it, what happens when you finally do shoot a big fish and it wants to take off on you? The shooting line is not very long and is attached directly to your speargun. You are holding the speargun. You are just about out of breath and need to go back to the surface for air. The fish is fighting for its life trying to get away while you try to swim to the surface. You are in a predicament.

If you hold on tight and try to pull the fish to the surface you might be successful. The other possible outcomes are not very good. If the fish is strong enough it can rip itself free from the spear. There's a good chance that an injured fish like this will die from its wounds shortly after escaping but it will be long gone before you can catch it. If the fish is strong enough and the spear is well embedded, the fish will pull you under until you either let go of the gun or run out of air. Both situations are bad for you.

The solution to this problem is something called a floatline. A floatline is a long cord that is attached to the very back of your speargun on one end and attached to a dive float at the surface at the other end. When a large fish is shot and starts to run, instead of pulling back on him and risk ripping out the spear, just let go of your gun and let the fish run. Now the fish is basically tethered to a very long line and an inflatable float at the surface. Take all the time you need to get back to the surface for air and when you swim over to your float you can take your time slowly pulling the fish to the surface. When he wants to run, let him run. Then pull him back when he gets tired. Pull back and forth using just enough pressure to bring the fish to you without risk of a pulled spear. Sounds better than being pulled underwater by a big fish doesn't it?

The length of your floatline will be determined by the depth that you typically dive. I generally recommend that your line be about two times the depth of your dive. I am usually comfortable diving to about 25 feet so I use a 50 foot floatline. The added length helps to resist the pull from your float at the surface.

A floatline can really be made out of any cord material so when you are just starting out something as simple as nylon rope will do the job. As you get more experienced you will want more from your floatline. The one that I use is a bungee style floatline that allows it to stretch much longer than its original size if necessary. It is made out of a 50 foot piece of green plastic surgical tubing with a 75 foot long piece of nylon cord in the center. The surgical tubing will stretch, the nylon cord will not. At a certain point the tubing will break but the nylon inner core will not so the cord prevents the outer tubing from stretching beyond its breaking point. This gives the whole line a rubber band or bungee effect. It is also sealed and attached to large swivel clips at both ends. This keeps it air tight and allows the line to float.

Another danger of pulling in a very big and still quite lively fish is the possibility of getting tangled up in your own floatline at the surface. As the fish swims around you it is important that you stay clear of any slack line and be very aware of your excess line and the way it is moving in the current at all times. Pull the line in so that it will float away from you as you get closer to your fish. This is where a floating line can be helpful. If the line sinks and starts to get all tangled up below the surface it can be very difficult to keep away from. Never underestimate the liveliness of your fish because as it gets closer to you it may all of a sudden wake up and make another run. Keeping your floatline clear of your body and free from tangles is very important at all times.

When you pull in a large fish the bungee effect of the floatline becomes more important. Again, you don't want to put too much pressure on the fish for fear of pulling the spear. With a floatline that acts like a rubber band, you can feel comfortable when the fish makes a run that the line will stretch to let him go a bit but give you just enough resistance to continue to pull it in. A bungee system makes it very difficult for a fish to escape.

Dive Float

Floating on the surface, attached to the other end of your floatline is your dive float. It is required by law to have a dive float and flag if you are spearfishing. The purpose is to alert boaters of your presence and to prevent accidents. The first float that I had was an old lobster trap buoy that I found washed up on the beach. I converted it into a dive float by adding a flag on one end and a weight on the other end to keep the flag upright. Again, with a little creativity you can make a dive float for very little money.

The float that I currently use is an inflatable, torpedo shaped float made by Riffe. It was a bit expensive but I thought it was worth it. Because it is inflatable, it can be stored in a very small compartment when it is deflated. It is weighted on the bottom and has a dive flag on top and it also has stainless steel rings on the front and back to clip things to the float. I usually attach three things to my float: the floatline, a fish stringer and an emergency whistle.

One of the best features of having a float is the ability to hang any fish you have shot from the stringer. This eliminates the need to take each fish back to the boat or to shore after you get one. Some spearfishermen have a stringer attached to their body or clipped to their weight belt. I don't like that idea because you are basically attaching bloody fish to yourself and asking for trouble. Keeping the wounded fish a significant distance away is a much smarter plan.

The Riffe float is made from a very durable outer fabric surrounding an inflatable center. It has a small blow up valve and a large deflating valve. If I were to give any negative criticism to this float it would be that the valves are sometimes faulty. When the air leaks from a valve while I am in the water it causes the float to slowly deflate and makes it roll over on its side in the water. Frustrating.

There are similar shaped dive floats available that are not inflatable. They take up a little more space while transporting your equipment but they have the advantage of never losing air and always staying afloat. Both types of dive floats are very positively buoyant and are very difficult to submerge. There are very few fish that can take a dive float below the surface after being shot. However, as you get more experienced, the pelagic species of fish like tuna and wahoo and amberjack may be in your sights. For these fish, a more advanced float system may be needed because some of these fish are strong enough to take a typical float underwater indefinitely.

Another advantage of the dive float and flag is to act as a signal beacon to your general location. Wherever your float is, you will be less than 50 feet away. The floats will often help dive buddies find each other while in the water. Last, but not least, your dive float can act as a rescue device in an emergency situation. Sometimes I use it to hold onto for a while to catch my breath and regain some energy. It is a secure feeling to have that life saver close by and ready when you need it.

Thus far we have discussed all of the basic equipment needed to get wet and get started in spearfishing. When you get more involved you will learn about some other gear that may heighten your experiences and help take you even further. In the next section I will review some accessory equipment that I use and find to be a big help while spearfishing.

Dive Computer

One device that I constantly use every minute that I am in the water is my trusty dive computer. Dive computers are used by SCUBA divers around the world because they provide information about a dive such as remaining air supply, temperature, location, depth, direction, bottom times, etc. It is an invaluable piece of equipment and no experienced SCUBA diver would go in the water without one. The spearfishing freediver however, may not need all of that information because there are no air tanks or regulators. The spearfisherman is going up and down all day on his own breath. As such, there are different pieces of information that are valuable to the spearfisherman.

When I am in the water I would like to know the temperature, the depth of my dives, the amount of time I spend at the bottom, the amount of time I spend resting at the surface and occasionally the time of day. For this information I used a dive computer that is the size of a large wristwatch. It is a wonderfully handy device made specifically for the freediver by a company called Suunto. My model may have been replaced by a newer version since its inception but it gives me everything I need while on the water. I'm sure any newer models will also provide the same information and then some.

A dive computer is a pretty expensive purchase but if you really take to this sport it is well worth the investment. Specifically look for something designed for the freediver. Suunto is a reputable company that makes all kinds of dive watch/computers but feel free to explore other companies as well.

In a later chapter on Freediving Techniques, I will describe in more detail how to use a freedive computer and why it is such a valuable tool to have. At this point however, know that it is not absolutely necessary for the beginner but it sure does help when you are trying to get better at spearfishing.

Other Accessories

As with most hobbies, I tend to accumulate "things" that go along with my activity. They may not come all at once, but over time the collection begins to grow. The accessories that I have may not be absolutely necessary for you but I will list them and describe the purpose of having such items.

Waterproof equipment bag: This is no more than a large duffle bag that can accommodate the bulk of my dive gear. It helps me keep things organized and portable. The length of your fins will usually dictate how long your bag needs to be.

Fish Stringer: This was briefly touched on earlier as an attachment to my float. My stringer consists of a two foot long piece of my shooting line (500 pound test monofilament) with a swivel clip on one end and a nine inch metal spike on the other. When I swim a fish back to my float I will spike it through the eye sockets to tether it to my stringer.

Knife: I rarely dive with a knife but some people say that this is a vital part of their dive gear and won't leave home without it. When I first got started I took a knife with me all the time. It was strapped to my leg for easy access. I can certainly see why someone would want to have one – just in case of emergencies. After going on countless dives without ever pulling it from the sheath however, I decided that it was not something I needed. I may regret that decision some day. I hope not.

Digital camera: There have been recent developments in underwater cameras that have produced some very small and very affordable models. I have one made by Sony that looks like a simple point and shoot pocket camera. After all, it is. But it is also so much more. I have been able to take some pretty amazing underwater videos of my adventures with this little camera. It is very impressive and relatively inexpensive in the $200 range.

Dive light: I will talk about night diving later in this book. My primary purpose for diving at night was to learn how to dive for lobsters. A good dive light is a bit expensive but it is essential if you are going to venture out into the water in the dark. Spare batteries are also a great investment to keep around when you depend so much on your light. The light that I own is called a Light Cannon 100 made by Underwater Kinetics. I have tried cheaper lights that my friends have purchased but nothing can hold a candle to the Light Cannon.

Lobster gauge: If you're going for lobsters, a lobster size gauge is a must have item. It is nothing more than a measuring device to make sure your lobsters are of legal keeping size.

Lobster bag: Similar to the function of the fish stringer, a lobster bag is basically a portable holding tank for your catch. I use a mesh bag that is attached to a Styrofoam round tube. It floats at the surface and I have it clipped onto my floatline so it moves along with me as I search for lobsters.

Spare weights: Sometimes you will need to vary your weight in order to get to the bottom. In stronger currents it can be difficult if you are struggling all of the time to stay in one place. Having a few extra pounds with you can make a big difference. Ankle weights are a quick way to add a few pounds in a pinch and help to sink your legs. Just don't add too much weight or you will find yourself expending too much energy to stay afloat at the surface.

Cost of basic equipment

I'm going to throw out some ballpark numbers that come from memory. This section is meant to be a guide. If you are a smart shopper you will find good deals online. Also, since my equipment was purchased a while back, you will most definitely find better bargains and technological upgrades today.

My initial wetsuit was a Henderson Gold series suit. I used a 3mm hooded vest underneath a full body suit that was 5mm thick. The wetsuit (called a jumpsuit) cost about $400 and the hooded vest was about $100. Gloves and neoprene booties made from Henderson added about $40 to the cost

After using that for a few seasons I did some more research and found that there were suits that were much better for freediving and spearfishing. This is when I purchased a custom fit wetsuit from Elios online. I thought the custom fit suit would cost more but surprisingly it was significantly less. After shipping (from Europe) and converting Euros to dollars, the suit, which included gloves and booties, cost about $250. I highly recommend this company and this type of suit because it is a much more comfortable fit and has a lot of stretch to the material which helps you breathe easier. There are a lot of choices when it comes to wetsuit material. The Elios company will ask you about the general environment that you hunt and make some suggestions for you.

A starter weight belt can be very inexpensive – around $6 for a nylon belt with a plastic buckle. Lace through lead weights will cost a little less than $4 per pound. About 15 pounds of lead and a belt will cost about $60.

The next upgrade in a weight belt system would be a rubber belt with metal buckle which costs about $25. Vinyl coated lead weights are a little more than $4 per pound. This system suited me very well for years until I lost my belt. That is when I started looking into weight vests that distribute the weight to your shoulders more than just your waist.

The weight vest that I found at the time cost about $100 and the soft weight lead shot bags cost a little over $3 per pound. I use about 18 pounds of lead so this system cost me about $160.

Masks can vary in price quite a bit but a smart shopper can get a very good mask for about $50. I have spent close to $100 for masks that I thought were worth it. If you buy online make sure there is a good return policy because there is no substitute for trying the mask on your face and testing the fit and comfort. Also get a little bottle of defog gel for about $5.

A good snorkel will cost about $20 or less. If you buy into the snorkels with all the bells and whistles like I did originally, you will spend about $40 or more.

A good set of fins that will last you a long time will cost about $120. If you believe you can get by with a cheapo set of fins that you find in a mask/snorkel/fin combo pack then you can spend about $20 on fins. I do not recommend this. If you are serious about spearfishing, plan to spend a little more on your fins. You will not be sorry you did.

My Riffe speargun, which is a Competitor X Series, costs about $400 brand new. I was lucky to get mine used, but still in excellent condition so I didn't pay that much. Proficient underwater hunters are continually upgrading their stock so finding good deals on used spearguns is not too difficult.

You do not have to get a Riffe when you start out. There are many other brands and models available and you can probably find a good deal on a starter speargun for around $200. Just keep in mind the things that I discussed in the speargun section of basic equipment.

Spare powerbands which are premade will cost about $20 each. A spare spearshaft will cost about $60.

I bought a floatline from a guy that makes them out of his garage. I was referred to him by a fellow spearfisher and that is probably the best way to purchase equipment. My 50 foot bungee float line cost me $50 but after going online to see what they cost new I found similar lines for well over $100. All that being said, you can get a nylon rope for next to nothing.

The dive float that I started with was a converted lobster buoy that I found on the beach. I added a $5 dive weight to the bottom and I was spearfishing. When it came time to upgrade to a Riffe inflatable float, I spent about $125. Looking back on it now it seems ridiculous to spend that kind of money on a dive float. Was it worth it? I'll say 'yes' with a little bit of hesitation in my voice.

If I were to start up again right now from scratch I would probably spend $50 on an inflatable, torpedo style float from amazon.com that comes with a 60 foot float line. You get what you pay for so I wouldn't expect the quality of such an item to be top of the line but to just get in the water and get started this is a good deal.

A spike style stringer will cost about $16. An emergency whistle to clip onto your float will cost about $3. Now we're talking. Much more reasonable.

A little less reasonable is spending at least $300 on a wrist watch dive computer. This is what I spent for my Suunto D3 several years ago. Maybe they are less now but there's a good chance they are more. The information this will give you is well worth the investment. Maybe wait a year or so like I did before making this purchase. When you finally do get it you will ask yourself why you didn't get it right in the beginning.

Underwater cameras, in general, are a very expensive item to purchase. I found this little handheld model by Sony that takes really good video for about $250. It's not great video – just really good considering the cost. Again – well worth the investment if you want to look back on your adventures some day. If you're just in it for the fish, skip this purchase.

A stainless steel knife and sheath with leg straps will cost about $30 but you can really go nuts with this item and spend well over $100.

Lobster diving opens up a whole new set of purchases. The Light Cannon 100 will cost about $250 and don't even ask what it costs to replace the bulb if it blows out. 8 C batteries for the Light Cannon are not cheap either at around $12. Double that if you want to have a spare set. A lobster gauge is only $2. A lobster holding bucket will cost about $15 if you can find one.

A fairly decent mesh dive bag to tote all of your stuff will cost about $40. Or you can get a jumbo nylon duffle bag for about $16.

Equipment Cost Estimates

wetsuit	$200
gloves	$25
booties	$25
weight belt and weights	$60
mask	$50
snorkel	$16
fins	$100
speargun	$300
float and float line	$50
stringer	$16
whistle	$3
total of necessary equipment	$895
dive computer	$300
camera	$250
dive light	$250
batteries	$24
lobster gauge	$2
lobster bucket	$15
dive bag	$20
total all equipment	$1,756

Ok – there's your investment. I'm sure I missed a bunch of things but from my perspective this is going to be the cost for the basic equipment to begin the hunt. If you have a friend who spearfishes there is a good chance that he has a bunch of spare stuff lying around. Do your research, borrow what you can, buy the basics and get wet. Figure out if this is something that you will enjoy. If so, this list is probably just the tip of the iceberg. However, I have been able to get by for years on just the equipment listed above with very little need for upgrades or replacement.

Sources for equipment

Having a dive shop nearby is always a plus when it comes to getting the equipment you need. As I have already mentioned, there is no substitute for being able to try before you buy. Although I have not taken advantage of it, there is a dive shop near my home that has an indoor heated pool attached to the shop. They are able to function all winter long giving lessons and letting people sample their equipment. Now that is a great idea.

Having a friend who can act as your mentor and dive buddy is also one of the best sources for equipment. I have learned a lot from several people who are more experienced than I am and I have taught a lot of what I know to friends who are less experienced. What goes around comes around. I am fortunate to have a small sport fishing boat and when I was just learning to spearfish I was quite popular amongst the spearos in my area who were boatless. They used me for my boat and I used them for their knowledge. It was a mutually beneficial relationship and it was a way to bring people together who shared a common interest. I can't say enough about learning from others who are willing to share what they know and what they have to offer.

Besides dive shops and friends, probably the most popular place to acquire your dive equipment is from online retailers. I have compiled a brief list of online dive shops and other retailers that I have used for some of my equipment purchases.

See Appendix A at the end of this book for a list of online resources.

Cleaning and maintenance

Once you've made a significant investment in your new hobby, it will be important for you to know how to maintain your equipment. Salt water can be very damaging if it is not thoroughly rinsed off. I try to make it a routine to fill up a tub with fresh water and dunk everything I used for spearfishing that day right into the tub. Anything that won't fit gets hosed off. After a good soaking I hang up my wetsuit, gloves, booties, mask, weight vest, etc. to dry. The sun is wonderful for drying my wet stuff but also realize that you do not want to leave your things out in the sun for too long. Once it is thoroughly dry, put your equipment away and out of the sun. Too much sun and too much salt can degrade your equipment over time.

Some people use a soft soap to wash and soak their wetsuit in. If you use it frequently, the neoprene will start to smell funky. It doesn't hurt to use a soft soap from time to time to wash your suit. It is not necessary to do every time but I would base my decision on how it smells and how often it gets used. When you purchase your wetsuit ask your vendor if there are any specific instructions for the particular materials used in your suit. Ultimately this will be your best source to find out the cleaning and maintenance requirements.

After my mask has dried I put it right back into the original hard plastic case that it came in. I can rest easy, when my dive bag is being thrown around, knowing that my mask and glass lens are safe and sound in the case. This is another good habit to get into.

Occasionally the teak on the speargun will need to be treated with oil to freshen it up a bit. I don't care too much for cosmetics so I'm only rubbing my speargun down about twice a season. The oil really has a way of rejuvenating the wood and making it look new again. It also helps the wood resist many of the harmful effects of prolonged sun and salt exposure. If you keep this wood in good shape it will last a very long time without warping, chipping or cracking.

There is not much maintenance for the floatline after it has been rinsed and dried. I neatly coil it up and put it in the bag for the next time it's needed. The terminal ends have stainless steel clips on them to resist rust. Pretty much every exposed metal in any of your equipment is made from stainless steel for the same reason.

If you end up getting a dive computer like the one I have, you will need to change the battery once a year. This requires a little care just to make sure the battery compartment is sealed water tight with a new O-ring each time it is opened. In fact, the Suunto company has a spare battery kit that comes with a battery, an O-ring and a new battery compartment cover. They don't want you taking any chances. If a plastic thread on an older screw-in battery cover has been compromised from being replaced over and over it can lead to a water leak. Salt water and electronics do not get along very well. The company wants you to protect your investment by replacing all of these components whenever you replace the battery. It makes perfect sense.

Chapter 3 – Where to Go Spearfishing

Now that you have your basic equipment it's time to get wet and start exploring the sea. The ocean is a very big place and it is mostly an underwater barren wasteland. A very small percentage of the ocean is inhabited by fish so where do you get started? A good initial solution to this problem is to become very familiar with your own back yard. Your back yard consists of the bodies of water that are closest to you and most easily accessible. If you're anything like me then you have been fishing in your home waters for some time now and have a pretty good understanding of the environment. If not, then it is time to start exploring.

As previously discussed, one of the best ways to get to know a new body of water is to have a guide, friend or mentor show you the ropes. Many people are protective of their favorite spots so don't expect to see them right away. It takes a lot of trust to get into the inner sanctum of a fisherman's secret spots. And don't expect to get something for nothing either. If you are expecting someone to teach you something they know, be prepared to reciprocate that favor in some way that will be beneficial to them. An example I gave earlier was an invitation to come aboard my boat in trade for some experience and advice.

If you are outside your home body of water the use of a paid guide service may be expensive upfront but the knowledge you gain will be well worth it. Whenever I go fishing in a new area or vacation destination I almost immediately look to a professional guide that is intimately familiar with the local waters. When your time is limited in a new area you want to make the most of it. Pay someone to show you around on the first day and spend the rest of your time exploring the productive waters that you learned about. Otherwise you could end up wasting a lot of valuable time and ultimately a lot of money trying to find spots on your own that may not be there.

Spearfishing is still a relatively new water sport so it may take some time to find the right type of guide. Ask the right questions and find someone who is eager and willing to take you by the hand and teach you what he knows. The trade off for him is that he will be paid for his services.

Visual cues

For now, let's stick to our home waters and learn the basics of finding the right places to dive. Fishermen, as said earlier, have a good jumpstart here. If you fish then you already know where some of the fish hang out. It doesn't matter if you are in a boat or off the shoreline somewhere. Fishermen find spots and will repeatedly visit these same locations time after time when they are productive.

Fishermen use visual cues to identify fishy locations. For example, a flock of gulls wildly flapping and diving near the surface is usually an excellent visual cue that there are some predator fish nearby. The gulls have visual cues of their own. They are keyed into the smaller baitfish that have been balled up and driven to the surface by the larger fish underneath. It is no fun being a baitfish in this scenario because they are being attacked from below and from above. When the baitfish eventually disburse or disappear, so do the working gulls and so do the fishermen.

Like the fishermen, the fish that we are after are mostly the predator fish – the ones with some size and some meat on their bones. So the first lesson to be learned here is to key into visual cues of productive water. The visual cue for the spearfisher is to look for fishermen. They have already done most of the time consuming dirty work. They have spent countless hours exploring from place to place and have decided to focus their attention on particular areas of interest. It is rare that you will see a group of fishermen in an area if none of them have ever caught a fish there. There are very specific reasons for them to be there in that location and at that time of year. We will get into this more in a later section but keeping a diary or logbook of your experiences will be a valuable asset to you in the future. Keep a log of locations where you see people fishing and make sure you track the dates. Many fish cycle through areas on a regular basis at specific times of the year. These are called 'runs' and it is very helpful to know when a species of fish is going to have a run based on historical data.

Another visual cue that is helpful to the spearo is structure. Fishermen also key in on structure and it has proven time after time to attract fish. The word structure has a very broad definition in the fishing world. It can literally mean anything that isn't water or sand. In trying to explain why fish are attracted to structure you will need a very basic understanding of the underwater food chain. The most basic idea here is that small things eat smaller things but are eaten by larger things. This chain starts from the tiniest microscopic piece of plankton and goes all the way up to apex predators like the great white shark. Sometimes these teeny tiny microbes just float around in the open ocean – but that would make them an easy target for whatever is feeding on them. So the small stuff in the sea prefers to congregate in areas where it can hide and protect itself from the next larger thing coming along. Wherever it can hide, like behind a rock or inside a sunken ship, is called structure. But guess what? The other fish know about this. You see, structure is a visual cue to larger ocean dwellers that smaller ocean dwellers are hiding nearby. The tiny shrimp finds the algae on the coral, the tiny crab finds the shrimp, the little squid finds the crab, the little fish finds the squid, the bigger eel finds the fish, the bigger fish finds the eel, the tuna finds the fish, the seal finds the tuna, the shark finds the seal. This underwater food chain is constantly refreshing and most of it centers on the areas of the sea that contain structure. Structure is where the tiniest microbes can attach and grow and where the little guy can hide from the big guy – or so he thinks.

Structure is also found in many places along the shore line. Docks, bridges, rock piles, mussel beds, boats, coral reefs, weed beds, shells, trees – all structure. These are the visual cues that will let you know where to start looking for fish in your home waters. From experience I know that I see many more fish when I am near structure than when I am in open water.

Another helpful tool for the spearfisherman is a topographical map of the area. This is particularly helpful when fishing from a boat but can also provide a lot of information about the shore line as well. If you are in a boat that has a GPS mapping unit for navigation, you will be able to look at a topographical map of the area to find favorable places to drop in. These maps show depth contour lines so that you can target specific depths that you prefer to dive. Additionally, fish also like to congregate in areas along the bottom that have abrupt depth changes. They like to come up to the shallows to explore and hunt but feel comfortable with the safety of the depth nearby. These are called drop offs and are another popular visual cue for the spearfisherman to pay attention to.

A topographical map will show the drop offs and a depth finder or sonar unit will confirm if you are in the right spot. I will often study a map prior to going out on my boat and target a few drop offs that look like they may be fishy. It's all part of the exploration and learning experience. Sometimes what you find is a desert wasteland and sometimes you feel like you drop into an aquarium full of life. Sometimes you can go back to the very same spot that was productive one day and it is barren the next. This is where your log book comes in handy again. Learn to always chart where you have been so that you can use it as a personal reference guide for future dives.

The bottom of the sea

After you have located some potentially fishy areas it is time to start exploring underwater. If you remember back in the beginning when I described the basic premise of spearfishing, go to the bottom and become a rock – all of the action is at the bottom. I like to swim to the bottom and locate an actual rock and grab hold of it to help me remain as motionless as possible.

"Why the bottom," you may be asking. This is somewhat of a secret that the average rod and reel fisherman may not know. In fact, if regular fishermen are reading this book, this is a section to pay close attention to. Where there is structure (rocks, coral, shells, etc) there are most likely a host of filter feeders attached to the structure. Remember the food chain. It starts with microscopic plants and animals floating around and also attaching to structure where available. You don't see these microbes individually but when they proliferate, what you see is a cloudy mess. More appropriately is what you can't see. When there is an algae bloom or when there is an abundance of microbes floating about, the water becomes dirty. Dirty water is a nightmare for a spearfisherman. It makes it virtually impossible to hunt.

The filter feeders include, but are not limited to the bivalves like clams and mussels and scallops. Think about a bed of mussels covering a rocky bottom. All of the food particles that get washed through this zone by the current are getting eaten by the mussels. And in the process, the water is getting filtered. Measured from the sea floor upward, the zone of filtered water is about 4 feet high. This also depends on the quantity of filter feeders in a given area but for the most part wherever there is significant structure on the bottom, there is a 4 foot zone of relatively clear filtered water. This zone is the fish highway.

Remember also that my "back yard" body of water is the Northeast coast of the United States specifically New Jersey and Rhode Island. These are my familiar waters. Some days when I dive it is extremely clear but these days are rare. For the most part, the visibility where I dive is about 10-20 feet in any direction. Some days are better, some days are worse. Occasionally it looks like it is going to be a great dive and after I gear up and get in the water, I can't even see the end of my speargun. These days are a total bust. Visibility plays an important part in how successful a dive will be. Paying attention to the weather, tides, currents and dive locations will help you determine if the visibility is going to be acceptable.

I don't have the luxury of jumping into the tropics like the Florida Keys or the Virgin Islands where the visibility can be 200 feet! Where I live, the water is dirty and dark. Where I live, I need to find the zones of clear water or else there will be no spearfishing. I need to find the filter feeders and the fish highway.

I call this area the fish highway because most of the fish I see are traveling in this zone. I believe that the fish just naturally prefer to swim in clear water over dirty water. Sure, fish have senses well beyond ours when it comes to underwater life. But one of the senses they rely on is sight and just like us, it is easier to see in clear water than it is in dirty water. How can this be disputed?

When I am sitting at the bottom in a relatively clear zone I can look up above my head and view a layer of haziness that I cannot see through. When I see fish they are almost always cruising just below this layer of haze. They are traveling. They are taking the fish highway from one place to another and they are attracted to this zone because within it their vision is not impaired.

Something that differentiates the spearfishermen from rod and reel fishermen is the fact that by using a fishing rod and bait or lure, they are trying to elicit a feeding reaction from the fish they are after. The fish they catch either need to be hungry or instinctively lured into eating or attacking. We, the spearos, are simply entering the realm of the fish in a relatively non-threatening way. We see where they live and gain their trust by being quiet and still. By doing so, we gain a better understanding of their home and we start to become aware of the types of environment to find the fish we are after. This is how I know about the fish highway and this is why I fish on or near the bottom whenever I fish with a rod and reel anymore.

I'm sure there are frequent exceptions to this. When the water is clean from top to bottom the filtered water doesn't seem to be much of an issue. When the predator fish have driven a school of baitfish to the surface in a frothing frenzy, the clarity of the water doesn't seem to be much of an issue. However, these exceptions are rare. Visiting these fish where they live and commute on a regular basis is the most reliable way to achieve success.

Another advantage of being close to the bottom is hidden within the basic body design of the fish themselves. The typical fish is dark colored on top and light colored on bottom. This is nature's way of camouflaging the fish and protecting them from predators. If you look down from the surface at a fish it blends into the darkness below. If you are below a fish looking upward toward the surface, its light underbody blends into the brightness from above. Both situations make it difficult to see fish that are directly below or above you. However, when you and the fish are on the same level they are quite easy to see. Fish that you never knew were there suddenly appear as if from thin air. You can see their eyes, their stripes, their colors, their fins and their tails. Since most fish are near the bottom, traveling along the fish highways, this is the level where you need to be in order to easily see them. Make sense?

Of course, not all fish are created equal. Knowing as much as you can about the particular species you are hunting will also increase your chances of success. Some fish like a sand bottom while others like a rock bottom. Some swim constantly while others lay motionless. Some are more curious than others and some fish will never easily be seen because they keep their distance. In the next chapter I will discuss the popular fish species that I target in the Atlantic Northeast and how to approach each one differently.

Chapter 4 – Species of Fish

While most of my experience is in the Atlantic Northeast off the coast of New Jersey and Rhode Island, many of the techniques described in this book can be used for fish species around the world. As long as you have a basic understanding of the type of fish you are after, you can modify your approach to gain a tactical advantage in their environment. There are a handful of species that I target for the purpose of putting some fresh fish on the table. In this chapter I will share what I know about these fish and offer some insight on how to hunt for them.

Striped Bass

skill needed	moderate	(beginner, moderate, advanced)
taste	4	(1-5 Bad to Excellent)
size	4	(1-5 Small to Large)
difficulty	2	(1-5 Easy to Difficult)

The primary fish that got me interested in spearfishing is the striped bass. Striped bass are attractive to me because they taste very good, they can get quite large and they inhabit the waters near my home in decent numbers for most of the year. Over the past 20 years striped bass have made a significant comeback in our area. This is due, in part, to the efforts of conservationists who placed size and catch limit restrictions on the species when they noticed it was in decline. Today, recreational fishermen have to adhere to these restrictions or suffer a significant penalty. Spearfishermen too, must adhere to all of the same legal size and catch limits that are in place and observe any changes to these regulations each year – for all species.

A big striped bass is a prize to take home. Anything over 30 pounds is a real trophy and anything over 50 pounds puts you into an elite class. These fish feed on a very wide variety of sea life including small worms and bugs, clams, crabs, lobsters, squid, eels, small fish and large fish. Sometimes they are very aggressive feeders and will churn up a frenzy on the surface of the water. Sometimes they are lazy, opportunistic scavengers that feed on pieces of fish left behind by other predators. It all depends on their mood and how much competition is nearby I suppose. Striped bass feed during the day but are also known to be nocturnal feeders which is why many fishermen target them during the night. The big, smart ones (known as cows) are most likely feeding in the dark and scavenging during the day on easy to catch prey. There's a reason why they got to be big after all.

The benefit to the spearo is that we don't have to worry about enticing these fish to eat. It's helpful to know what they eat because if you find their food source you will increase your chances of finding them. But basically, we just have to find out where they commute back and forth to work every day. We have to learn where they like to hang out and then stealthily drop in on them. This is not always as easy as it seems.

Striped bass are curious cruisers and are often found in small to medium sized schools. Typically, similarly sized bass seem to school together. It's rare to see very small fish mixed in with larger ones. I presume that they travel and grow together and stay fairly close to their peers throughout their life. Striped bass will swim around you in wide circles if you have the ability to stay under long enough. The quieter you are, the tighter the circles will get and you can feel them curiously staring at you. If you are patient you can be very selective and almost pick out your fish as if you are at a seafood market. If you start to get anxious around these fish the circles get wider and it becomes much more difficult to target a specific fish.

If you find yourself in a school of striped bass it is common to see them all get startled at the same time. When this happens, they all turn and you will hear an underwater thumping sound that their big broad tails make in unison. If you remain still, the school will come back because of their curious nature. This sound can sometimes be heard even when there are no visual signs of fish around. Because sound travels easily through water, it is important to listen for these cues that can alert you to the fact that there may be a school of fish nearby.

Many of the schools I have encountered consist of medium to large fish in the 20 pound range. This size is excellent to catch and eat and is well within the legal limit for keeping this species. Whenever I am targeting striped bass however, I am really looking for that one big trophy fish. The cow. Several of the big fish I have encountered behaved quite differently from their medium sized counterparts. When striped bass get over 30 pounds they start to look a little different. Their heads are bigger and broader and their belly gets fatter. It's almost like seeing a different fish altogether. It's hard to describe but when you encounter this for the first time you will know what I mean. The big cows, although I'm sure they school together occasionally, seem to be more solitary than the smaller bass. The ones that I have come across have just been lazily cruising along the fish highway. Not as curious as the younger ones – as if to say that they have seen this all before and are just on their way from here to there. When you see a fish like this, be ready to take your shot because you may only get one chance. They are not going to be hanging around very long.

Striped bass are really beautiful creatures. They have a series of unmistakable black stripes from head to tail across their silvery sides. They have big, broad, powerful tails and very large, toothless mouths. They inhale their food whole and use muscles in the back of their throats for crushing. Their flesh is mostly nice white meat and has a very mild flavor. Although the striped bass is a formidable prey, once you get the hang of the basic spearfishing techniques they are not very difficult to hunt. Their curiosity is their downfall and because they don't have too many natural predators they are not too wary of the presence of strangers in their neighborhood.

Blackfish (Tautog)

skill needed	beginner
taste	5
size	3
difficulty	1

Blackfish are the best target practice for the beginner spearo. They have a curious nature, similar to the striped bass, but they are much more abundant. It seems almost everywhere I dive where there is structure, there are blackfish present. These fish are not cruisers going from place to place all the time. They are tuned into the structure because that is their source of food. Unlike bass, which can be found almost anywhere in the water column, blackfish are primarily bottom dwellers. It is very rare to see a blackfish venture very far off the sea bottom. They prefer very rocky areas because they use the rocks for protection and shelter. The rocks also provide them with a great source of food – mussels.

If you find rocky mussel beds along the bottom you will most definitely find blackfish. They love chomping on mussels all day long and their mouths are built for it. Blackfish are pretty strange looking when you get up close and personal. They have odd looking front teeth that protrude out of their mouths. As their name implies they are mostly dark brown or black along their sides and back and as with most fish have a whitish belly. They are also known for having a pretty white chin especially as they get larger in size. Blackfish are typically about 3-5 pounds with the really large ones pushing 10-14 pounds.

There are usually small ones mixed in with larger ones so the spearfisherman must be aware of the size limits before shooting a blackfish. Underwater, your mask has a tendency to magnify things. It is important to take this magnification factor into consideration especially when you are just beginning. It's easy to mistake a fish that looks large enough underwater only to bring it to the surface and find that it is quite smaller than expected.

Blackfish are great table fare. Although they are somewhat ugly, pretty slimy and bony, they do clean up well. They yield thick white fillets that hold up quite nicely in fish soups or chowders. They are not a very oil fish so they lend themselves to sautéing and frying as well. Blackfish is a very popular food fish and as such it has some pretty stringent restrictions and catch limits.

Blackfish are not very difficult to obtain. They have a curious nature and that keeps them relatively close to you while on the bottom. You can sometimes poke away the smaller ones with the tip of your spear. The larger ones are a little more cautious which makes them more of a challenge. Often times, blackfish are so numerous that it is difficult to focus on just one fish. This is the power that fish have in schools against larger predators. Try to focus on one fish and follow it with your spear until the best shot is lined up. The temptation is to be swayed to change targets because you see a bigger one out of the corner of your eye. This happens often and with time you will learn which fish to shoot.

Another advantage that the divers has over the fisherman is the fact that he is able to pick and choose the fish that he takes. Some people look at spearfishing as being cruel and barbaric but we are typically harming many less fish than the average fisherman. There is virtually no waste or unnecessary killing of fish. It is rare to kill fish that are not of legal keeping size. While fishing, occasionally small fish are hooked in their mouths or gut in such a way that ends up killing the fish – even if it is released. As long as the spearfisherman has good morals and stays within the legal limitations for the fish he is after, there is usually no collateral damage. In these ways, spearfishing is more conservation minded than fishing with a hook and line.

Fluke (Summer Flounder)

skill needed	moderate
taste	5
size	3
difficulty	4

One of my personal favorites to eat is the fluke. These fish yield a fine, white flesh that lends itself to an endless variety of cooking techniques. If cleaned properly there are usually no objectionable fishy smells. I prefer my fluke breaded and fried but my wife likes it broiled with a nice garlic butter sauce. Either way, we know we are in for a treat when I bring home some fluke.

Fluke are quite unusual looking. Related to flounder, halibut, sole and other flatfish, fluke have both of their eyes on one side of their heads. They are called flatfish because they are usually thin and flat and lie on the bottom. Fluke are dark brown and have blotchy, spotted skin on one side and are white on the other side. They camouflage themselves by burying their bodies under a layer of sand. Flatfish look upward with their eyes protruding through the sand and wait to ambush their prey as it swims or drifts past them. It is a very effective hunting technique - not all that different from what we are doing underwater.

Fluke can be somewhat difficult to hunt with a spear because of their ability to hide. They are not curious like the bass or blackfish and they typically do not cruise around a lot. Sometimes you can just barely see the shape or outline of their body beneath the sand. Sometimes they lie on the bottom and their coloration and spots make them blend into the surroundings. Many times you will be close to a fluke without ever knowing it and the second you get too close, it sees you first and quickly darts away. I will seldom go spearfishing with the intent to target fluke but every so often I will spot one while looking for other fish.

Once spotted, they are not too difficult to shoot but keep in mind that you are shooting right into the bottom. If the fluke is sitting on a rock or hard surface it can be damaging to your spear to fire, fully loaded into such structure. Larger fluke tend to prefer camouflaging themselves in rocky areas containing mussel beds, weeds and other debris. They do this because they are hunting too and are targeting the types of food that inhabit areas with more structure.

Fluke are deceptively aggressive predators. They have large mouths and an array of very sharp teeth used for grabbing hold of their prey rather than for chewing. Some of their favorite foods include squid, a wide variety of small fish, small crabs, and basically anything else that swims past them that will fit in their mouth. Fishermen catch fluke using rigs designed for bottom fishing with live bait as well as artificial lures. Fluke are not ultra selective and as such, they are very popular fish to catch.

I have to be honest and say that I am much more successful catching fluke with a rod and reel than I am with a spear. However, the largest fluke I have taken was shot with my spear while I was out looking for striped bass. This fish was buried under a whole bunch of bottom debris and it took me about three glances to realize that there was a big fish hiding under all of that stuff. I shot to what I thought would be the middle of the fish because all I could see was a tail coming out one side and some mouth parts coming out the other. This fluke turned out to be almost 9 pounds.

Fluke, on average, weigh about 2-4 pounds for a keeper and anything over 5 pounds is a pretty substantial catch. Fluke over 10 pounds are true trophies and these fish max out in the 20 pound range. A 10 pound fluke hardly seems like a trophy when their close relative, the halibut, can often reach 200 pounds or greater. Much of it depends on your location but a halibut behaves in a very similar manner to the fluke that I have described – just on a much bigger scale. Atlantic halibut inhabit much deeper colder waters. Halibut are also a very popular species to catch along the Pacific Northwest coast. Though not impossible to spearfish for these larger cousins of the fluke, just think bigger in all aspects of your equipment.

Bluefish

skill needed	advanced
taste	1
size	4
difficulty	5

The taste of different fish is somewhat subjective. I may really like a taste that others despise and vise versa. It also has a lot to do with the preparation. That being said, bluefish have always tended to be one of my least liked fish to eat. That's a good thing though because they are also one of the most difficult fish to shoot with a spear.

When I do catch bluefish, I make sure that I clean them really well. They are quite oily and have a streak of dark red meat which runs through their flesh. This red streak is very fishy tasting and needs to be completely trimmed from the fillets. Bluefish fillets are not really white like the other mild fish I have described. They are grey in color and have a very strong flavor. The oiliness of this fish lends itself well to smoking. This is how I prefer to eat bluefish but it can also be prepared in a number of other ways.

Bluefish swim in a similar pattern to striped bass. They are cruisers – constantly on the go. While bass curiously stick around for a while to check you out, bluefish are not interested at all. They are naturally skittish and very cautious underwater. In fact, it takes an awfully long, motionless breath hold before you even can catch a glimpse of a bluefish. And if you turn in their direction, they are gone in a flash – and fast too!

In contrast, bluefish are often quite easy to catch with a rod and reel. They are voracious eaters with a mouthful of ultra sharp teeth lined up in a row. Bluefish are choppers. They use their strong jaw muscles and teeth to rip apart their prey. They often feed in large packs and attack schools of baitfish with a sense of recklessness. Because they hack their food to pieces while eating, bits and pieces of fish parts will often fall from the surface to the bottom. This is where the large, opportunistic striped bass pick up the scraps.

Bluefish are very aggressive while eating probably due to the competition from other bluefish. This aggressive nature is what makes them easier to catch. Bluefish are often taken using artificial lures made out of shiny metal that mimics the size of the baitfish they are feeding on. When they are on the feed, they will eat just about anything you throw at them.

I have not yet experienced a full blown bluefish feed while spearfishing underwater. I have been close a few times but just as I seem to approach the school, it disappears. I'm not sure if the fish are alert to my presence but for whatever reason they are gone before I get a shot at them.

Bluefish get to a maximum size of around 20 pounds, give or take a few. A 10 pound bluefish will give you a great battle and pound for pound they are one of the hardest fighting fish around. Bluefish have a forked tail and a long, sleek, silvery blue body with, of course, a dark top and a white bottom. They are built for power and speed and with their sharp teeth and powerful jaws they are a force to be reckoned with in the water.

Porgy (Scup)

skill needed	advanced
taste	4
size	1
difficulty	5

Porgy are small, snapper-like fish that swim in schools and are usually no more that 1-3 pounds. They are pretty good to eat but because of their small size the amount of meat you get from each fish is minimal. They are also quite bony so after thoroughly cleaning there is only a small fillet left. It is a fine, white flesh that has a mild taste and can be prepared in a number of ways.

Porgy are worth mentioning in this book because they offer a pretty significant challenge for a spearfisherman. Similar to bluefish, they are very wary of anything strange in their environment and keep their distance. Porgy are on the dinner menu of the striped bass. Many fishermen actually use live porgy for bait to catch very large stripers and I have occasionally found them inside the bellies of bass when I clean them. As such, they need to be very cautious to avoid being eaten.

When porgy are around they are very plentiful. However, you could be underwater with them all around and never actually see one. They are like ghosts. It takes a really long bottom time for the spearo to begin to see porgy in the distance. After sitting very still for about 45 seconds you will just start to see a cloud of them emerge into your sights. This is why they are such a challenge. Not only are they a small target but they never get close enough for you to make an accurate shot. If you can hold your breath long enough however, you will be rewarded with some very tasty fish for your dinner table.

Triggerfish

skill needed	beginner
taste	5
size	2
difficulty	2

Triggerfish are not exactly common to my home area. However, every so often they will show up. Take advantage of it when they do because triggerfish are easy to catch and are delicious to eat. They are interesting looking fish and their skin is very tough, like leather. The triggerfish that I have seen have all been around 3-5 pounds but I know they do get bigger. They are somewhat tropical looking with a variety of colors in their skin and they are very bony with a unique spiny dorsal fin or trigger. This spine is part of their natural defense mechanism because when it is locked in the up position it sticks out like a long sharp thorn. If attacked or eaten by a larger fish this thorn would make it very difficult to swallow.

Triggerfish may have fewer natural predators because of their defenses. This could be why they are not as cautious as some of the other fish I have discussed. In fact, they are somewhat curious, bordering on stupid. Being poked with a spear doesn't seem to bother them very much. Being shot with a spear is a different story.

Triggers are usually grouped in small schools and when they are around you can usually get a few of them before they disappear. They don't get very spooked like some other fish after the speargun is shot in their vicinity.

Other species

In my back yard, the fish that I previously discussed are the primary food fish that are taken while spearfishing. Our waters are loaded with many other species of fish and sea life that are a little less common, but worth mentioning. Some can be harvested for food while others are there to be admired.

Some other food fish include: weakfish, black sea bass, flounders, kingfish, crabs, lobsters (to be discussed in more detail in a later chapter), clams and mussels to name a few.

Sea life I have observed underwater that I would put on the "do not shoot" list would include: small sharks, a wide variety of rays and skates, spiny puffer fish, pilot fish, bunker and other baitfish, eels, spider crabs, many types of jellyfish, starfish, sea urchin, squid and many more.

Remember, it is always an adventure when you go into the mysterious world under the sea. Admire its wonders and respect its dangers. The more often you go, the more confident you will get and the more comfortable you will be in this strange place.

Chapter 5 – Getting Wet

There are several ways to begin your journey into the underwater world of spearfishing and each one has its own advantages and disadvantages. When it comes down to it, your individual circumstance will determine which method is right for you in your specific environment. Let us examine in detail some of the most popular ways to start.

Shore dives

Not everyone has a boat or has access to one. Let me start out by saying you certainly do not need a boat to go spearfishing. I live in an area where it takes me about five minutes in my truck to drive to a beach where I can access some fairly decent water from shore. I can leave my house, get in the water, do my thing and be home with some fish - all within a couple hours. If the conditions are not great or the visibility is terrible I turn right around and go home without wasting my entire day. Some days when the conditions are very good I can be in the water within fifteen minutes of leaving my house, shoot a fish and be home within an hour. You can't beat that for convenience.

Everything I need for spearfishing I can fit into a giant duffle bag. From my parked truck it is a short walk to the beach, across the sand and to the ocean. I usually leave my bag on the beach or on a rock while I am in the water. I trust that no one passing by will steal my bag but there is not much in it while I am in the water so there is not much at risk. It takes me a few minutes to get into my wetsuit and gear and then I am ready to enter the water. This beach often has small to medium sized waves that I have to swim past in order to get to open water. Considering the fact that I am not going spearfishing if the water is too rough, these waves are pretty simple to get through. Almost immediately upon entering the water I can tell if the visibility is going to be favorable for spearfishing. It is rare, but a few times I have made it all the way to the water only to discover that I am unable to see far enough to make the trip worthwhile. In these instances it is best to just pack it in and wait for another day.

Choosing the right weather and water conditions is a learned skill that will take some time and experience to master. With the right knowledge and information you can start to identify the conditions that will make a spearfishing adventure successful and those which are not worth spending the effort. It is difficult to plan any type of fishing trip too far in advance because so much can be dependent on the weather. One advantage of a shore dive is that it has the flexibility of being a really short trip if the conditions are not ideal.

When I get the urge to make a shore dive on short notice, I immediately check a few trusty resources I have at my disposal. First, I check the inshore weather forecast online. The overall weather and temperature are a good start, but most importantly I am looking for wind speed and direction. I have found spearfishing to be best when the water is as calm as possible so we are looking at the forecast for conditions suitable for the calmest water. Light west winds keep the waves and chop to a minimum. Because I live on the East coast, a west wind blows from the land out to sea. The natural movement of the waves pushes them inland from east to west so if there is a light wind pushing from west to east it will cause these waves to diminish in size. When I read a report and it tells me there are east winds, I know that the wind is blowing in the same direction as the waves are moving. An east wind gives more power to the waves and they become much bigger and stronger.

The next forecast I check is the direction and speed of the currents and the tides. For my conditions to be as calm as possible I want there to be slow moving currents and slack tide. Believe it or not, the phase of the moon also plays a role here. When the moon is full, the high tides tend to be a lot higher than normal which means the current and movement of water is usually quite fast between tides. This is why it is important to try to time your dives close to the slack tide if possible.

Interestingly, this is quite the opposite if you are fishing with rod and reel. Fishermen usually try to time their trips so that the current is moving and not slack. The theory behind this is the idea that moving water tends to also move smaller baitfish and food particles in the current. Many fish are opportunistic by nature and prefer to expend as little energy as possible to pursue their prey. With the current moving they can position themselves in specific areas that make it easier to ambush smaller fish. It's like having a meal delivered to them rather than having to go out and find it. Fishermen have learned over time that predator fish are naturally more aggressive and willing to feed during times when the water is moving instead of when it is still.

Conversely, spearfishermen are not after the fish that are feeding. We are looking for fish that are cruising around on the fish highways going from place to place. Still water is our friend because it allows us to be as still and quiet as possible. It also helps us take better shots by not pushing us or the speargun around in the current.

When I have determined that the wind, current and tides are in my favor the next resources that I check are some beach webcams online. Webcams are popular these days and if you do your homework there's a good chance you will be able to find a beach cam that will give you a live picture or video of a nearby beach. There are a few in my area that I regularly turn to. Instantly I can see if the water is choppy or if it is calm. I have one that also shows a large flag in front of the ocean so this helps me to confirm information that I already know about wind speed and direction.

For quick, shore dives the internet can provide up to the minute information that can tell you if the conditions are right for spearfishing. Smartphones and other portable devices can easily allow you to tap into these online resources from wherever you are at any time. Many surf fishermen use the same resources to determine if their areas are going to be favorable for fishing as well.

The surf fishermen and the spearos have a very interesting relationship. I described earlier how we can use them to locate potentially fishy spots. Well, they can use us as a valuable information source too. Many times I have gone out spearfishing while there were surf fishermen nearby. A couple big advantages that I have are the ability to swim out way beyond their farthest casting distance and obviously the ability to see if there are any fish around. When I swim back to shore with a stringer full of fish, it gets some serious attention from anyone standing on the beach with a rod and reel. Just seeing this lets the fishermen know that there are fish out there to be caught. The attention often draws them near with a host of questions about what I saw underwater. I am very friendly with the fishermen because ultimately we are all sharing some knowledge in order to hone our skills and increase our potential for success. No one wants to waste their time fishing in a desert where there are no signs of life. If that's the case, I tell them. I will also try to direct them to areas where I have located underwater structure points like rocks or mussel beds that are within their casting distance.

This may sound a bit smug but it is always stimulating to me when I haul in some fish in front of surf guys who have been fishing all day without a bite. This constantly reaffirms my choice to venture out into the fish's domain and to be a spearfisherman. Too many hours and days I have spent sitting on that beach with a rod and reel, without a bite, wondering if there were any fish around.

Diving from shore does come with some disadvantages. In my area I dive from a sandy beach – emphasis on the word sandy. I'll just come right out and say it. . . I don't like the sand! When I finish with a shore dive I have to take extra care to clean all of the sand off my equipment. Then when I get home, again I find that I'm cleaning sand off my equipment. Then after it all dries, I find that I'm cleaning more sand off my equipment. There is no end to the sand. Even though there are very few mechanical or moving parts in the speargun, sand in the trigger mechanism can be a problem. Even the fish that I catch get covered in sand and it is a chore to clean it all off. Sometimes, after taking every precaution along the way to clean the sand off my fish, I'll bite into my dinner and still get a hint of sandy grit between my teeth. This is the pinnacle of frustration. Bottom line, if you are diving from a sandy beach, be prepared to wash, wash and wash all of your stuff when you are finished.

An advantage of a shore dive is that it costs little to no money – after your initial investment in your equipment of course. With rising fuel costs these days it can be quite expensive every time you take a boat to go fishing. Boats however, do have the advantage of being able to explore areas well beyond your normal fishing grounds. This is why some people look for a compromise and turn to using a kayak for spearfishing.

Kayak dives

Kayaks give you more freedom and versatility to travel much greater distances than if you were simply swimming from a shoreline. They may not offer as much freedom as a boat, but the savings in fuel expense may make a kayak a worthwhile investment. Also, kayaks can sometimes get into tight and shallow areas that boats cannot. So there are definitely times when a kayak has its advantages over a boat. Some spearfishing tournaments restrict the competitors by only letting them use kayaks to get around. This is a way to have a tournament and keep the playing field relatively even.

Kayaks are very popular among spearos. They can take the place of your dive float and you can conveniently attach your float line directly to your kayak. Most dive kayaks are sit-on-top style boats and have several storage compartments built into the hull for your equipment. Some people fully rig their kayaks with rudder systems, foot pedals, sonar and GPS electronics and more. A basic kayak however, is all you need to expand your back yard.

One disadvantage of a kayak is the fact that it is man powered or paddled. This is a necessary means by which you travel but it also causes you to expend a lot of energy. It helps if you are in top physical shape but if you are not, just remember that you will have to rest for a significant amount of time after doing a lot of paddling.

A kayak for the purpose of spearfishing should be a fairly stable vessel. You should be able to jump off and climb onto it with relative ease and it should be resistant to tipping. There is nothing more frustrating than expending exorbitant amounts of energy trying to get back onto your kayak only to have it continually tip over. If you are buying a kayak new or used, it is important to do an on-the-water trial to test this out. There is no other way to determine if you will be able to get off and on easily other than to test it for yourself. It may be a bit extreme but it will be worth it in the end. Conserving your energy is one of the primary objectives of a spearfisherman so do not take this step lightly.

I suppose it is time to reveal what happened to me in the kayak incident that I have made several references to. I was planning a kayak spearfishing trip one morning, intent to launch from a beach in New Jersey. This was my first time launching at this site and I took a lot of precaution to make sure I would be successful. The weather seemed fine. It was mostly calm with a few waves breaking here and there. I suited up and stowed as much gear as I could into the hatches of my kayak. On top of the kayak I had a bucket strapped down to the hull and inside the bucket I stored my gloves, mask, snorkel and weight belt.

I held onto my paddle and began to push the kayak into the water. When I got about waist deep, I hopped on board and started paddling out to sea. Inexperienced in the surf, I did what I thought was right and headed straight into the small breaking waves ahead. The first couple cut nicely through the bow of the kayak and I even floated right over a couple waves that didn't break. At one point, my kayak got slightly turned so that the bow was no longer pointed into the waves. Even though the waves were quite mild this day, a side facing kayak in breaking waves is a disaster waiting to happen. It was only a short distance more to paddle beyond the breakers but before I had a second to think, I had lost all control. I could not turn the kayak in the right direction and the next wave that hit my side flipped me over. What was originally planned as a beautiful day out on the water searching for fish, instantly turned into a disastrous salvage mission.

I never felt like I was personally in any danger. I was fully suited up and floating in the water where I had intended to be in the first place. However, I was now faced with the challenge of righting a flipped over kayak and trying to save any gear that I could manage to find. I knew right away my day was shot. I managed to first swim the kayak back to shore. This was no easy task as the waves in the surf are relentless. Even though they were small, they just kept coming. Over and over and over again. Every time I tried to turn the kayak in the right direction it was pushed back sideways and then flipped over again by the next wave series. The only potential danger was to be in the way of the kayak when a wave hit it. Wisely I stayed on the correct side but this position made it more difficult to bring it to the beach. It took several minutes and by the time I had the kayak on the beach, the current had pushed me about a hundred yards north of where I started.

I managed to save my speargun, floatline, paddle and anything else either attached to or stowed away in the kayak. Unfortunately, after spending a lot of time searching, I lost several pieces of equipment. The weight belt did a good job of keeping the mask and snorkel in the bucket but it also did a good job of sinking the bucket to bottom – lost forever.

Whenever I have a negative incident like that I try to make an effort (after some time has passed) to ask myself what I learned from this experience and, if anything, what positives came from it. I certainly learned a lot about launching a kayak through the surf. I learned how important it is to check all of the available weather, wind and wave forecast sources prior to going spearfishing. I learned that everything should be stowed away in hatches and to expect that the kayak will flip at some point. As a result of losing my weight belt I researched alternate weight systems like the weight vest harness – which I now believe I like better than the belt. I do regret losing my mask. I loved that mask and it wasn't cheap. I thought I would miss my snorkel as well but as it turns out, I was probably using the wrong type of snorkel for spearfishing. This event caused me to investigate other snorkels and now I use one that is less expensive and one that I truly believe has some significant benefits while breathing at the surface.

Kayak diving does have some risks but after you become comfortable with your kayak and your surroundings it can offer a lot more areas to explore than you could ever discover shore diving. Another thing I really like about kayak diving or fishing is that it is quiet. Having a stealthy approach gives you a significant advantage especially because sound travels so well through the water. Kayaks glide through the water making very little noise. The sound of a motor boat engine can be heard from a very long distance away. I don't know how much the fish dislike the motor boat sound but clearly there are benefits of having virtually no sound at all. Some fish are very skittish and the slightest disturbance can cause them to leave an area.

Boat Dives

Even with all the disadvantages discussed like fuel cost and noisiness, for me, boat dives still offer the best opportunities for spearfishermen. I am fortunate (for now) to own my own boat. It is a 19ft open center console with a T-top. For fishing and diving it is a great boat to have. It is small enough that I can easily trailer it around from place to place. I get relatively good gas mileage with a single 4-stroke outboard motor. I can go pretty far and pretty fast on one tank of gas. While diving, I can get in and out very easily without the use of a dive ladder or other assistance because the side hull is low enough in the water. Maintenance and repairs are even a relatively minor expense.

When you start to get even a little bit larger in size, the costs of having your own boat really start to add up. With a slightly larger boat you may have the added flexibility of exploring even further beyond your home waters as well as the ability to get there faster. You also get additional cabin space and areas to store your equipment and your catch. But other than that, there are few advantages that a larger boat will offer. Of course, the best possible situation is to have a really good friend who owns a boat and doesn't mind buying the gas.

Because this is a basic guide to spearfishing, we will stick with my small center console and discuss some of the ways in which you can use a boat to your advantage. Let's start by finding a particular area or spot to try spearfishing. My first inclination would be to use my on-board electronics. As long as your boat is large enough for a battery, it is capable of having a sonar and GPS unit. In my opinion, this is a 'must have' item for any boat owner because it is an invaluable tool for both function and safety. Don't leave home without it. It's not even worth discussing the particular unit that I have because next month there will be a new one out with different features. I spent about $700 for the unit I own. It is by no means the top of the line product in this industry but for what I use it for, I can't complain. I would basically suggest looking for a sonar-GPS combo unit if you are in the market for this type of electronic and want to get the most for your money. The companies, Lowrance and Humminbird have relatively inexpensive models while names like Garmin and Raymarine are higher in the price scale.

At the time I am writing this, there are some really cool developments in technology with smartphones and tablets like the iPhone, iPad and the Android models. Most of these devices have a built-in GPS and it makes sense that the developers of fish-finder electronics would take advantage of this. There are applications (apps) for these devices that give you a pretty accurate GPS map of the water. This technology is only going to get better and better so if you are on a tight budget, in the near future you may be able to save some money on a combo unit and get your GPS information straight from your phone or tablet device. This might bring up issues like waterproofing and charging and other problems but I'm sure there will be ways to improve on these areas as well.

No matter which unit you work with, the GPS map is going to be your starting point. We talked earlier about finding a spot to fish so once you have your location in mind, follow your map to get there. Once you get relatively close to the area you want to dive, switch over and start to read your sonar. In addition to finding fish, we use this more importantly to look for bottom contours, depth and structure. I usually ride back and forth very slowly over a potential fishing area a few times so that I can be sure I am in the right spot. I will also turn off the engine and drift for a short while so that I can get a feel for the direction and flow of the currents.

One of the biggest advantages (maybe THE biggest) of diving from a boat is the ability to spearfish in a moving current. The current will tell me a lot of information like how fast I am going and the general direction I am likely to be heading. If the current is strong, my dive plan is going to be much different that if there is weak or no current. I discussed the benefits of slack tide when diving from shore. When you are in a boat, slack tide can be treated just like a shore dive. Go to your location, drop an anchor and jump in. At slack tide you can swim near the boat, up, down, all around and no matter where you end up, you have a relatively easy swim back to your boat where you left it. The dive plan is simple – go as far as you want but know you have to swim the same distance back to the boat.

It would be my preference to always dive at slack tide and plan the timing of my trip accordingly. When diving from a boat it is usually a half or full day of fishing so throughout that day the tide and current are constantly changing. It's nice to take advantage of the slack current when available, but you should also know how to manage best as the water starts to move.

When you are in even a slightly moving current you will notice it fairly quickly. First off, when you throw the anchor in and it catches bottom, notice how long it takes for the slack in your anchor line to pull tight. Also, how tight or loose is the line? These are indicators for you. When you jump into the water and just sit there motionless, is the boat getting further away? How fast? Make a mental note of these things. I am often very excited to jump into the water and get started fishing on my very first dive of the day. It is easy to overlook these indicators but try to resist this temptation. Never underestimate Mother Nature and always mind your environment. What appears to be a normal calm day on the surface may be quite a different situation under water. Also know that this is a dynamically changing environment throughout the day. What holds true for one hour may be significantly different the next so keep in touch with your senses and make mental notes of the changes as they happen. Even better, learn how to anticipate the upcoming changes based on weather forecasting and tide charts and other information that you gathered prior to your dive.

Two experiences come to mind when discussing diving in a mild current. Both are unpleasant. I will share them so hopefully someone can learn from the mistakes that I have made in the past and prevent a potential problem in the future.

I was diving with my friend Greg. We were both relatively inexperienced and just happy to be in the water searching for striped bass. We anchored up and jumped in together. The conditions were really good. I was showing Greg a few things about equalizing and some techniques I use to get a better bottom time. We shot a few fish, had a good time and we weren't really swimming very much. We were just floating, catching our breath, talking a little and diving to the bottom. Up and down. Up and down. When we got a little tired we decided to take a break and head back to the boat. The only problem was, the boat was really, really, really far away! How did this happen? We were barely swimming.

We were both inexperienced in minding our environment. The current had been moving us slowly enough for it to be somewhat undetected but quickly enough to take us quite far. I just lost track of time and didn't keep a close eye on the boat. Your general proximity to the boat will usually give you a good sense of how strong the current is.

The dangerous part about this experience was the fact that we had to swim back to the boat. We were already tired from our dive and the current was against us. Oh, and if I forgot to mention it, I had 18 pounds of lead around my waist and I was pulling about 20 pounds of fish on my float. Not a fun swim. Another funny thing about being the one who owns the boat is that other people don't really care as much about getting to the boat as you do. So guess who did most of the swimming?

Well, we actually wised up in this particular case and decided it would be best if only one of us (me) swam for the boat. I left Greg behind but took advantage of the situation by leaving him floating with my weight belt, speargun, float and fish. I still had to swim against the current but it was a much easier swim without the extra weight. I try to remember this situation every time I do a boat dive and make it a habit to swim into the current when I start. After I get in the water I will simply follow the direction that the boat is pointed and swim right out in front of the anchor line. This way I know how difficult it is to swim against the current right away. Also, when I get tired of swimming, I can then relax and do a few passive dives and let the current sweep me right back to where the boat is anchored. Lesson to be learned: mind your environment and keep one eye on the boat at all times.

My second bout with an unpredictable current was a little scarier. This time I was out with a friend who was also a dive instructor. Man, he should have known better for sure! We were checking out some interesting spots along a rocky shoreline in Rhode Island. I anchored the boat in relatively shallow water on the edge of the main channel that connects the ocean with Narragansett Bay. We both got in the water and headed toward the rocks to look for some fish. The slight current was moving across the channel into the main deepwater harbor so the swim back to the boat should have been a breeze. We expended some energy going against the current to get to the rocks and then settled in to relax and begin the hunt. The contour of the shoreline was a winding array of rocky cliff-like formations that we swam around as we ventured further away. I swear I was looking at the boat every chance I could but sometimes my vision was obstructed by the rocks.

Suddenly, I got a very good look at the boat and it was really, really, really far away. My friend was a little further along than I was and seemed oblivious to the situation at hand. I immediately realized what had happened. The anchor had pulled loose from the bottom. This caused the boat to drift out into the much deeper channel where the anchor line was too short to even come close to the bottom.

Funny thing about being the one who owns the boat - other people don't really care as much about getting to the boat as you do. Guess who did the swimming? I had to make a split decision in this circumstance because my buddy was in one direction and the boat was continually drifting further away in the opposite direction. I couldn't easily get to him to discuss the situation so I started to swim for the boat. Luckily I was swimming with the current but working against me was the fact that I wasn't able to drop off my weights and equipment with my buddy. Let me tell you something. Don't try to win any swim races with 18 pounds of lead strapped to your waist. Several times I contemplated tying my weight belt to my floatline and just dropping the weights. It seemed the more I swam, the farther away the boat kept moving. I think the wind was also pushing the boat along in the same direction which added to the difficulty.

After several minutes I paused to take a good look around and I found myself floating in the middle of Newport harbor channel in about 120 feet of water. This channel is a shipping lane for big tankers, cruise ships and even military air craft carriers that travel to the Navy base inside the harbor. This is no place to be swimming – let alone wearing a dark camouflage wetsuit. I had to drop my weights and equipment and kick this swim into another gear. I really had no other option at that point. I attached my weight belt to my floatline and let go of my speargun. The float had plenty of buoyancy to stay on top even with the extra pounds pulling it down.

I took a risk by dumping my equipment but in the end it had enabled me to get to the boat more quickly. Once in the boat, I hauled up the anchor, picked up my float and gear and headed back to my "buddy" who was still oblivious and had no idea that anything had happened. At least that's how he reacted to my story but come on. I had a hard time believing that a dive instructor would be that ignorant of a potentially dangerous and significant event. Needless to say, it was the last time I went diving with that guy. Lesson to be learned: You can pick your friends and you can pick your nose, but you can't pick your friend's nose. Wait, sorry, that was a different lesson. How about this one: Mind your environment, keep one eye on the boat at all times and make sure the anchor is secure!

For moving current, the dive plan changes and this is where your buddies come in handy. To really make the most of a day while diving from a boat, having at least three people is a definite advantage.

Earlier, I mentioned my friends Greg and Pete. This is a perfect example of taking advantage of having three people on board. We already know that it is vitally important to have a buddy in the water with you at all times while diving. Right? With three divers, two can be in the water while the other one takes a rest and manages the boat. This is the best situation.

I would use the three person advantage with Greg and Pete whenever possible. The best strategy starts with locating a particular site you want to dive. Using my electronics we would pinpoint a target location and drive right on top of it to confirm the depth. Once we knew that the depth was within our diving skill level we would turn the boat off and drift for a short while. In the prior example we were using the anchor and when the anchor line pulled tight we would get a good read on the direction and strength of the current. While drifting however, we have to use our electronics and our senses. It doesn't take too long to figure out the general direction of the current while you are drifting. We would also use this time to gear up and get ready for the dive.

Pete starts out in the boat while Greg and I prepare ourselves. Once we are ready, Pete slowly circles around to position the boat slightly up-current from where we located our spot. This is the drop in point. Greg and I know that we do not want to expend any energy to get to our target. By positioning the boat and dropping in up-current, we will be swept right over our spot after entering the water. The speed of the current will give us an indication of just how far up-current to drop in. If our target area is small, we may only get a couple quality dives in this location. Larger areas will allow us to drift further and cover more water each time we dive.

The best thing about the three person advantage is the fact that one man is always in the boat. He is typically just drifting along in the same direction waiting for a pick up signal by one of the divers. Greg and I have the freedom to conserve our energy by not swimming against the current. We can make several dives to quickly scout a particular area. We do not have to continually pay attention to where the boat is. Psychologically, this is also an advantage. Constantly bobbing your head up and down causes stress on your mind and believe it or not, this will inhibit your ability to relax and concentrate on your breath hold. I can focus on my breathing and my buddy. He can do the same keeping an eye on me. When either of us get tired or need a break, Pete is ready to swoop in for a pick up and to trade places.

Often times we will find an area that we sweep over fairly quickly. This enables us to change positions more frequently. The boat man would pick up both divers and make several quick passes over a spot. Additionally, if a spot proves to be unproductive, this method allows us to cover a lot of ground until we do start to find the fish. Even if the current is slow moving or slack, having at least three people still has the same advantages.

Another method of trying to pinpoint a particular spot is to drop a buoy overboard once you have located your target area. Attach a weight to the end of a cord that is long enough to reach the bottom. Ideally you would have two buoys attached to the other end of the cord – first a small one and then a larger one. The idea for the double buoy system is to assist the diver in re-locating a specific area and to provide information about the current. By watching the buoys and knowing that the larger buoy is always trailing the smaller one, the diver can determine the general direction of the current and make adjustments while in the water. It is very difficult to get your bearings while in the water because there are usually not many reference points to focus on. This is especially true for open water dives where the shoreline is not visible or close. When you are in the water you don't have the advantage of the electronics anymore. Using a buoy system as a visual cue will really help you locate the general area that you originally intended to hunt.

Although you can probably see the advantage of using a buoy system, it also has the disadvantage of needing to be picked up when it is time to move. This is not a huge problem but it can be a bit of a nuisance if you are planning on moving frequently from spot to spot.

Another thing worth mentioning in the discussion about diving from a boat is to make sure that you have the ability to get back onto the boat when you are in the water. I mentioned that I dive from a 19 foot fishing boat where the side walls a low enough to the water to enable me to get back on the boat. I give a good strong kick and grab a metal rail which I use to help hoist my body in. It's not exactly easy and I am used to doing it because I have practiced it several times. I know exactly where to grab and how much energy I need to get that initial surge out of the water.

Greg is a bigger, heavier guy than I. I didn't realize that he would have a much more difficult time getting back onto the boat until it was too late. Not only is this frustrating for him but it drains a significant amount of energy. The solution to this problem is to make sure that you are capable of getting back on the boat with relative ease and minimal struggle. Any boat larger than mine will require some additional assistance to get back on board. Many boats have either a dive platform or a swing out ladder in the back of the boat for divers and swimmers. There are also dive ladders that are designed for climbing out of the water with your fins on. I had one of these for a while but it was not very practical for my boat.

The three man advantage can also be helpful if a diver has difficulty getting back onto the boat. A helping hand is very welcoming to a tired diver who is struggling. Keeping one man in the boat at all times will assure that there will be assistance when needed.

Chapter 6 – Freediving and Spearfishing Technique

The equipment checklist

Get ready to start diving. There is no substitute for formal training by a qualified instructor or mentor but this section will give you insight on some of the techniques used to get to your fish.

You have picked your day, time and location and you are ready to embark on your adventure. This may sound redundant, but the first step is to gather up all of your equipment and do a quick inventory. Initially it will be a big help if you make an actual written checklist. I can tell you there have been several times that I have skipped this step and have been very sorry I did.

One day I was very excited to make a shore dive. I checked all of my online resources for the weather, tides, wind and current. The conditions were perfect. I usually keep all of my equipment in one place so I don't forget anything. I gathered it all up without doing an inventory check and loaded it into my truck. It was a relatively short drive to the beach and without hesitation I carried my gear across the sand and down to the water. It took some time to get dressed in my wetsuit, prepare my mask, uncoil my floatline, rig the speargun, set my dive watch, put on my gloves and fins and gradually move into the water. I tried to conserve my energy by slowly swimming out into the ocean and by breathing deeply as I went. My spot is about 200 yards off shore so I typically ball park this distance before going down for my first exploratory dive. This is the point where I realized the critical piece of equipment that I forgot. I didn't have any dive weights!

In my haste to get to the water, I forgot that I had hung my dive weight vest up on the wall next to my gear bag. I never noticed that everything seemed lighter while carrying my equipment from the truck to the water. I was just blinded by the excitement of going out spearfishing. This was the worst possible time to realize my mistake. Up until this point I hadn't needed my weights.

I tried several futile attempts to get below the surface but I had to franticly kick and struggle the whole time and as soon as I stopped kicking I would bob right back up like a cork. There was no questioning the buoyancy of my wetsuit that day. Even when I got underwater, I had expended so much energy that I couldn't hold my breath for very long. I don't even know why I tried but after going through everything I did to get out there, I had to at least make an attempt. Disappointed, I made my way back to the beach to call it quits. I just didn't have the desire to go all the way back home to get my weights after that experience. I learned from it though. I learned to make a checklist, either mental or preferably written, and to go through my pre-dive inventory so that each piece of vital equipment is accounted for.

Here is a quick list for reference but you will want to create one that is customized to your situation and equipment:

- mask and snorkel (and some type of defog liquid)
- fins
- wetsuit: top (with hood) and bottom
- booties
- gloves
- speargun
- floatline and dive float with flag and whistle
- weight belt
- fish stringer
- dive watch or computer

This is the bare minimum that I like to have for a dive. Some people would also include a knife in this list. Depending on the type of wetsuit you have, you may need some type of lubricant like soapy water, in order to slide your wetsuit on. Other things that I include in my dive bag are spare parts just in case something breaks.

Common spare parts:

- mask and snorkel
- spear shaft and shooting line
- lead weights
- watch batteries
- power bands

Gather up your equipment and head for the water. Suit up - it's time to get wet. By whichever means you plan on getting into the water (shore, boat or kayak), let's assume that you are now in the water and ready. You are fully suited up head to toe, lying on the surface and breathing through your snorkel. Your weight belt or vest is on, you are holding your speargun in one hand and attached to the back of the gun is your floatline which extends some distance behind you. At the end of the floatline is your dive float with a fish stringer dangling off of it and a dive flag sticking straight up. I also like to tether an emergency whistle to my dive float – you never know when you will need it.

Loading the speargun

It may seem obvious that the power bands need to be stretched over the barbs on the spearshaft but until you get used to the technique, this can be a bit tricky – and exhausting. I typically use three, fairly heavy duty power bands. If you use multiple bands like I do, you will always load the band closest to you first and typically put this band on the barb that is closest to the spear tip. Each subsequent band will go onto the next barb so that the bands lay evenly on top of each other.

The best way that I have found to load the speargun is to get as much leverage as possible by sticking the butt end of the gun into my belly or chest area and reach over the top of the gun to grab hold of the first band. With both hands pull back on the band and stretch it until you are able to get the band clip or cable over the barb on the shaft. This can take some practice and patience. Try to not get overly exhausted and carefully load one band at a time. A nice feature of many spearfishing wetsuits is a loading pad positioned on the front chest area. This is merely a thickened area of wetsuit material intended to absorb the pressure of loading your speargun. Without it, you may have the tendency to wear away a hole in your suit from continually jabbing the butt of your gun into the same area to load your bands. This pad also provides some protection to your body from the force and pressure that it takes to load your gun.

A word of caution: Once you have successfully stretched the first band onto the shaft barb, your gun is live and loaded. Even if the remaining bands are not stretched yet, your gun can be fired at this point and is potentially a very dangerous weapon. When diving with other people around it is very important that you don't point your gun in their direction while loading. Conversely, make sure that you are not in the line of fire of any other divers who are loading their spearguns. As a form of regular practice, a loaded or unloaded speargun should never be pointed in the direction of another person. This may seem like common sense but is worth mentioning for the sake of safety.

The first several times you load your gun it is normal to get a very sore spot in your belly or chest area. As you continue to practice and use your loading pad, you will get much more proficient at this technique. Over time it will become second nature and you will be able to load all of your bands in a very short period of time. I like to get all three bands loaded as fast as possible so that I don't expend too much energy and so that I can quickly begin relaxing at the surface in preparation for my dive.

Relaxing at the surface

With your gun loaded you are just about ready to dive down and look for some fish. With everything you have done at this point to get ready, your muscles have been working hard. Your blood-oxygen levels have been drained and need to be refilled. If you were to take a deep dive right away, you would only be able to stay underwater for a fraction of your maximum capacity. Your oxygen supply would diminish rapidly and you would have to come up quickly for air. This is why it is important to develop a relaxation routine at the surface in between each dive. By optimizing your oxygen supply, you will be able to go deeper, get much longer bottom time and dramatically increase your chance of catching a fish.

When I first started out in spearfishing I was very anxious to get to the bottom where the fish were. I didn't pay much attention to something called the 'surface interval' which basically means how much time you spend at the surface between dives. When you dive too quickly you run out of air more quickly. This becomes very obvious even for the beginner. I started to use my dive watch in order to establish a few rules that would help me refill my oxygen during the surface interval.

After a dive I would refer to my watch to see how long I was underwater. Then I would make sure that I stayed at the surface for at least two times that amount before heading back down. For example, if my dive time was 30 seconds – I would have to spend at least 60 seconds at the surface. Without any other relaxation technique, this simple timed surface interval served me very well and is a good rule to stand by. If you are having trouble refilling your air supply in this amount of time, try three times your dive time as a surface interval. The time may vary from person to person but having a watch and a timer becomes an invaluable tool during this part of your dive. When fish are present it is very difficult to stay at the surface for a long time. It takes some discipline but sticking to this rule will pay off in the end.

So what do you do while you are just laying there on the surface waiting for your interval to be over? Well, first off, don't think of sharks. It's really hard not to think of sharks when you are floating motionless on the surface of the ocean dressed up like an injured seal. Inevitably, you will think of sharks. There is just no way around it. Over time, as you get more accustomed to the waters you fish and see that there are no sharks to speak of, you will think of them less and less. This is easy for me to say as I sit and write these words but the reality is that the potential for sharks is always there. The other reality is that more often than not, any shark will be more afraid of you than you are of it. You are also not on their dinner menu so unless it's a case of mistaken identity you should not be in any danger of being attacked by a shark. There are special circumstances that may occasionally challenge that last sentence however – so no matter what I say in this text there may always be a very slight chance of an encounter with a shark. That is part of the danger of spearfishing. For some people that adds to the excitement of the sport. Personally, I would prefer to never see any one of the big three (white shark, bull shark or tiger shark) while spearfishing.

It's easy to get sidetracked on the subject of sharks and probably not the best thing to bring up in a section titled 'Relaxing at the surface.' But in the interest of keeping it real, the shark factor is something that does creep into your mind during the surface interval. This is detrimental to you in many ways. Mostly, if you let the anxiety of the shark factor get the best of you, you will not be able to relax on the surface. Your mind will be racing, you will constantly be looking all around, your heart rate will speed up and your ability to conserve oxygen will diminish. All of these things will cause you to need much longer surface intervals and limit your time on the bottom looking for fish. Let's move on though – there's a lot more to cover on the relaxation technique at the surface and if you practice keeping your mind on the next section, the thought of sharks will be minimized.

Surface breathing

Breathing through your snorkel is not the most efficient way to exchange CO_2 for oxygen. Every breath out will leave a snorkel filled with CO_2 that will invariably be inhaled on the next breath. This is why snorkel use may not replenish your oxygen as quickly as out of the water breathing but it is the best option that we have at our disposal at this time and it allows the diver to lay face down and motionless in the water while relaxing.

Breaths at the surface should be slow, methodical and relaxed – all intended to minimize oxygen consumption by the muscles in your body and lower your heart rate. An excited mind and a fast paced breath will use up a lot more oxygen. This is the time to slow things down to a crawl. When you get better at this part of the dive, you will see dramatic results. But - with anything, it takes practice and patience.

Start by practicing out of the water. Take a deep breath in, hold it in for two seconds and then let it out slowly. The breath in should take about 3-4 seconds and as you let it out, try to prevent it from going all out at once. You should try to lengthen the time of your exhale to about ten seconds. In order to do this you will have to use your tongue, lips and teeth to limit the amount of air that is released. When you first try this, make a hissing sound like a snake or like air that is slowly being let out of a tire. While you exhale, count to ten in your head. After ten seconds and all of the air has been released, hold again for two seconds before repeating the cycle with a big inhale.

During your surface interval it is helpful to have a breathing routine – something that you can remember and easily repeat time after time with relative ease.

Recovery/Relaxation Breathing Cycle
1. Inhale (3-4 seconds)
2. Hold (2 seconds)
3. Exhale (10 seconds)
4. Hold (2 seconds)
5. Repeat for your desired number of cycles

This cycle takes about 18 seconds to complete. Five cycles takes about 90 seconds to complete. That's a minute and a half of relaxation breathing. After a while you will start to get a feel for how many cycles you will need in order to have a surface interval that is at least twice as long as your dive time. For example, if I am getting about 1 minute dive times I want to do at least two minutes of relaxation breaths during my surface interval. 120 seconds divided by 18 (rounded up) tells me that I will need about 7 cycles before my next dive.

- 27 sec dive time = 54 sec surface interval = 3 cycles
- 36 sec dive time = 72 sec surface interval = 4 cycles
- 45 sec dive time = 90 sec surface interval = 5 cycles
- 54 sec dive time = 108 sec surface interval = 6 cycles
- 63 sec dive time = 126 sec surface interval = 7 cycles
- 72 sec dive time = 144 sec surface interval = 8 cycles
- And so on.

Relaxation breathing cycles will accomplish several things. First of all, it will help take your mind off sharks. Continual counting and trying to remember which cycle you are on will help keep you focused. It will also help to slow down your heart rate and re-oxygenate your blood and your muscles.

You are almost ready to dive. After completing your desired number of cycles, the last thing to do before taking a big breath in, is to purge as much residual CO_2 as possible from your system. One way to do this is to do a series of powerful exhales. Practice this by taking a quick, deep breath in (1-2 seconds) followed by a powerful release of all of your air (lasting about 4 seconds).

- Quick, Deep, Inhale (1-2 seconds)
- Forceful Exhale (4 seconds)
- Repeat 4 cycles

I know all of this seems very controlled and scientific the way it is timed and counted. These numbers and cycles are to be used as a guide and a reference for a beginner but once you get more experienced, a lot of this will become second nature. Even as an experienced diver you may find it helpful to look back at this section and revert to your prescribed number of cycles and counting schemes from time to time. It becomes easy to forget that your surface interval needs to expand as you begin to increase your dive times.

After purging your residual CO2 your body is now at its peak. You are ready to take in as much oxygen rich air as possible and ready to dive. Don't feel like you have to rush right into your big breath immediately after the purge. Just ease into it. Take a couple more normal, comfortable breaths and then you will be relaxed and ready.

The one big breath

Have you ever heard of something called 'the mammalian dive reflex?' It's a little too involved to go into at great length in this book. But what is important to know is that we humans, as mammals, have an inherent ability to stay submerged under water for extended periods of time due to physiological changes that occur when our faces get wet. Particularly in water colder than 70 degrees, when our faces submerge it triggers a series of events that are designed to keep our bodies alive as long as possible without air. Our heart rate immediately slows down and the blood vessels that go to our extremities will constrict. Our body automatically goes into self preservation mode and is trying to keep the most oxygenated blood as close to the core and vital organ systems as possible. By pumping more slowly, the heart is conserving as much energy as possible and slowing down the whole system.

As freedivers, we are taking full advantage of the mammalian dive reflex just as our distant cousins, the whales and dolphins have been doing since the beginning of time. In addition to what happens automatically at a physiologic level, we have just learned how to physically get ourselves into a state where we are ready for an optimal breath hold. Everything we've worked for up until this point has been in preparation for the one big breath that is going to fill your body and muscles with enough oxygen to keep you underwater as long as possible.

I'm sure you didn't think I was going to simply say – Ok, now take a deep breath and go under. No. Just like everything else, there are certain techniques to the one big breath that will help you get the most out of it.

The one big breath can be practiced at home or in a swimming pool or anywhere really. If you want to get the most out of it however, it's important to go through all of the prescribed cycles of relaxation breaths in order to lead up to the one big breath. Assuming you are doing some training at home, try holding your breath using a variety of big inhalation methods. Mix it up a bit to see what you are most comfortable with. Some examples may be: one large quick inhale, a long slow deep inhale, a very calm normal breath inhale, etc. Try only using your mouth and not your nose as your nose will not be available to you in the water.

For me, I have found that normal calm breathing, followed by an unusually long, pushing exhale, followed by a somewhat calm, longer than usual, extremely deep inhale – does the trick. Everyone is a little different so that is why it's important to practice to see what is most comfortable for you.

One thing I do feel is important to mention is way that you use your body to inhale. After winging it for several years and taking my big breath in the most comfortable way I could, I had a dive instructor show me a better way to use my body to get the most out of my breath. A few simple changes made a dramatic difference in the amount of air I was able to take in. There are a few chambers in your body that can hold air and if you take your breath in with the purpose of maximizing the air in each of these sections you will enhance your capacity.

The first area is your belly. For a few seconds, lie on your back on your couch at home and watch your belly as you breathe. Focus on making your belly rise and fall as far out and in as possible when you breathe. Take a big breath in and expand your belly out until you can't take in any more air. Now take in more air but instead of expanding your stomach, focus on expanding your chest. Feel the upper part of your lungs expanding to their maximum as you lift your chest up high. When you reach your maximum chest capacity, raise your shoulders up and back and find a way to inhale more air but this time into your extreme upper chest and neck area. When you've filled up this section and feel again as if there is no more room for any more air, stretch your neck out and head up high and fill your mouth and throat with the last amount of air you can find. That is the one big breath!

It is important to focus when you are transitioning from the first, belly chamber to the second, lung and chest chamber. It is easy at this point to allow a lot of the air that you took into your belly to escape into your lungs. So keep in mind that only the air coming in through your mouth is supposed to be filling your lungs. Although it is normal to have your full belly fall a bit during this first transition due to muscle contractions, do your best to minimize the flow of air from your belly to your lungs.

The big breath pathway
1. Belly
2. Chest and lungs
3. Neck and throat
4. Mouth

When you get the hang of this four stage big breath it shouldn't take too long to complete the whole process – about 3 seconds. Take your time in the beginning and concentrate on air flowing into each section separately. Soon enough, it will all flow together without much pause between sections.

This inhalation technique will most certainly allow you to hold your breath significantly longer than you have been able to do in the past. Practice it. Test your breath hold limits at home with a stopwatch. Typically, when you practice a breath hold while sitting on your living room couch (called a static breath hold) you can anticipate that you will get about half that amount of time while diving (dynamic breath hold). The reason for this time difference is the fact that your muscles are active while swimming and this causes a drain on the oxygen levels in your body.

Pike position

When it's time to make your dive underwater you should be thinking about two things – body position and equalizing. As you complete the stages of the big breath it's time to bend your body into the pike position. Pike position is a common term in gymnastics and high diving – sports which require the athlete to position their body in such a way to prepare for a flip, turn or general change of direction.

Point your arms down toward the bottom in the direction you are diving. Get your butt up high out of the water. As you lunge your body and chest downward, your legs will naturally flip upward. After your body begins to straighten out, start to kick your legs and head toward the bottom. Although your head wants to naturally tilt back so that you can view the direction you are heading, try to resist this urge by tucking your chin into your chest so the top of your head is pointing straight down. This is one of the most difficult things to remember during the pike position dive. However, if your head is bent back your body will slightly follow this angled trajectory backwards toward the bottom. It is a more efficient, direct path to the bottom if you are going straight down and ultimately this will increase your bottom time.

Time to start equalizing

As soon as you get your legs kicking to propel your body below the surface, it's time to start equalizing. As a rule of thumb, you cannot start equalizing too soon or too often. Refer back to the section on Pressure and Equalizing to review the basic technique. With one hand carrying your speargun, your other hand is free for equalizing. I happen to be a left-handed shooter which makes it very easy for me to use my free right hand without having to switch back and forth. I suppose a right-handed shooter will make adjustments to use his left hand for equalizing.

Just prior to equalizing for the first time, use your free hand to remove your snorkel from your mouth. Failure to remember this step will cause a negative pressure to build up in your mouthpiece as you descend. The snorkel has an air space that is sealed by your mouth and if it is not equalized or removed it will feel like your mouth is being sucked into your snorkel – not comfortable. Simply remove it and then bring your hand to your nose to start equalizing.

Some techniques may differ from person to person but I feel like a continual, rapid fire burst of equalizing about one time per second works best for me. This rate can be slowed down a bit as you gradually glide into a slow descent to the bottom. It can't be stated enough how improper equalization can ruin a day of diving. If you dive down past a depth that should have been equalized, you can risk serious injury to your inner ears and sinuses. It may be slight overkill to equalize as much and as often as I have suggested but for the beginner, it is important to figure out which method is most comfortable and safe for you.

The descent to the bottom

As you continue to equalize throughout your entire descent the next thing to focus on should be a very relaxed swim to the bottom. Because both of your hands are occupied, your leg muscles will do most of the work. However, instead of doing a lot of powerful kicking, it's time for your extra long freediving fins to prove their worth. A gentle, smooth kicking motion will activate those long blades and effortlessly propel you downward to the bottom.

Heavy kicking at this point will get you there faster but there will be a price to pay. If you rely on using big leg muscles to propel you through the water, it will cause your heart to pump harder and the oxygen in your body will drain faster. The 5 seconds you saved by kicking hard to the bottom will most likely cost you 15 seconds or more of bottom time as you will have depleted your air supply prematurely.

As you descend deeper and go past your neutral buoyancy point, you will begin to sink. You can really relax your muscles at this point and try to conserve as much energy as possible. The energy you want to spend should be concentrated on your equalizing. Frequent equalizing can be mentally taxing and can also cause a slight loss of air as you regularly push outward. Another thing to remember as you go deeper is the fact that the air space in your mask is being compressed. You will feel this in the form of outward pressure on your face and in particular, it feels like your eyeballs are being sucked out. If you don't do something to correct or equalize this pressure, it can be painfully uncomfortable as well as dangerous.

The way to combat this dilemma called mask squeeze is to add more air into this compressed space. When you equalize, release a little finger pressure on your nose and let a slight bit of air escape into your mask. You will immediately feel relief from the squeeze. This will cost you a bit of oxygen but it is a necessary evil for the sake of safety and comfort. In my experience, mask squeeze starts to take effect when you get to about 35 feet below the surface – give or take 5 feet. This is the depth at which you will need to borrow a little lung air to refill what has been compressed. The depth at which this occurs can also be dependent on your experience level as well as your particular mask.

Professional freedivers combat the effects of mask squeeze by using small goggles with very little air space. Even then, the eyeballs will still get a bit sucked out so to go one step further, some people eliminate this air space all together by filling their goggles with water. Obviously this will negate some of the benefits of goggles in the first place but when you are trying to contain every last bit of air, this is the way to do it.

As spearfishermen, we need to have the best underwater visibility through the glass in our masks. Filling it with water would be a mistake. We use a mask instead of goggles so that we can combat the mask squeeze by letting a little air back in.

There is a side benefit to releasing some of our precious air into our mask and I will discuss that later in a section that talks about the ascent to the surface after you have held your breath as long as possible. Can you figure it out?

Continuing to descend, as you approach the bottom and hopefully have favorable visibility, it's time to untuck your chin, cock your head back and glide into a horizontal position. Picture yourself like an airplane coming in for a smooth landing. Very little kicking is needed and assuming you have properly adjusted your weights for buoyancy control, your descent to the bottom should be passive, well controlled and as effortless as possible.

Adjusting weights for buoyancy control

The only time you can truly test your buoyancy and weight system is in relatively deep water. You may have to adjust your weights throughout the day if your dive consists of areas with varying depths. Ideally, your weights should make you neutrally buoyant after you descend to the halfway point of your dive. There is no exact formula because again, it depends on the particular depth you are diving as well as the type of wetsuit used. When you get beyond the neutral buoyancy depth you will start to fall freely toward the bottom with no effort at all. Only experience and testing will tell you exactly how much weight you should have.

I have tried a few different weight configurations over the years and I am still trying to figure out what works best for me. As an example, I frequently dive from the beach knowing that the depth I am targeting is between 16 and 25 feet. I also use a pretty buoyant, 5mm wetsuit. I want my weights to keep me pinned to the bottom when I am deeper than 15 feet but I don't want them pulling me underwater when I am trying to rest and relax during my surface interval. I require a pretty significant amount of weight to keep my body on the bottom preventing my wetsuit from floating me up – especially in relatively shallow water. I can achieve this goal with about 18 pounds of lead strapped to my body. This amount of weight is a little taxing on the surface but I am still positively buoyant – barely.

If I know that I am going to be diving in depths of 20 to 30 feet I can adjust my weights by removing about 6 pounds for a total of 12 pounds. This certainly makes it a lot more comfortable for me at the surface. And anything over 30 feet I can adjust down to about 10 pounds of lead. If I try using an amount less than 10 pounds I have a hard time kicking my legs to get my body deep enough to pass my neutral buoyancy point. If your lead is too light you will expend an unnecessary amount of time and energy and oxygen trying to get neutral. It's all about balance and sometimes you will need to make spur of the moment adjustments. After several dives you will gain enough information and experience about your weight system to be able to make the adjustments needed for your particular situation.

As a general rule, try not to be underweighted. If you do not bring enough weight you will be struggling to get below the surface. This can be very frustrating. If you bring a few extra pounds and find that you are sinking a bit at the surface then it is fairly simple to drop some lead until you are comfortable. A dive buddy can be very helpful when trying to figure out your weight system. You can have a buddy hold onto your extra weights as you determine a balance that works best for you.

Bottom time

When you figure out your ideal amount of weight it will be easy for you to hold to the sea bottom without expending much energy. In many locations that I have gone spearfishing I have found it important to be as still as possible while laying on the sea floor. By acting like a rock and remaining as still as possible you not only conserve energy and oxygen but you will also be less spooky to a variety of fish species. The longer you are able to stay still in one spot, the better chance you have of attracting the curiosity of the local residents. Some of this depends on the particular type of fish you are targeting. If you are generally in the right neighborhood however, most fish will be a lot friendlier if you do not move around and do not appear threatening.

Everything previously discussed about your breath hold, relaxation techniques and oxygen conservation has led us to this point. It was all designed to get you the longest, most comfortable time in potentially most productive spearfishing zone. Without contention, your chances of getting a fish get better and better the longer you are able to stay on the bottom. Knowing this simple fact, your goal as a spearfisherman should be to study and practice ways in which to increase your bottom time.

One way to practice is to work on breath holding times at home. Using a simple stopwatch, go through your relaxation breathing cycles and then time your maximum breath hold. Rest a bit and then do it again and try to beat your previous time. After doing this several times you will be surprised how you can push yourself out further and further. If you want to get a little more advanced, there are some computer applications that can assist you at home with breath hold training. They can keep pace for you automatically, time your rest periods and keep track of your progress. Of course, these are typically static breath holds so you have to remember the general rule that you might only achieve about half of this time while diving.

Another way to practice getting longer bottom times is to use a swimming pool if you have access to one. First try some underwater static breath holding by simply lying in the shallow end of the pool and dunking your face in the water. The water will naturally induce the mammalian diving reflex and hopefully provide some additional physiological assistance to increase your times. It may be a good idea to use your mask and snorkel for this training in order to accurately simulate a real dive.

The next way to make use of a swimming pool is to fully gear up and make use of the deepest part of the pool. This will give you a more dynamic breath hold simulation and is probably the closest you can come to open water dive training. Most swimming pools will only be about 12 feet at their deepest point. Residential pools are even less. If you plan to do dynamic pool training with full gear, you will need to adjust your weights accordingly. Most likely you will need to add a significant amount of weight in order to hold bottom in 12 feet. Of course this can make it quite uncomfortable at the surface. To combat this you can use a ladder to hold onto or some type of floatation device while you try to relax at the surface. Another way to adjust your buoyancy is to remove some or all of your wetsuit and this way you can use much less weight and still hold bottom.

Competitive freedivers sometimes go one step beyond swimming pool training in order to find deeper water to practice their skills. A man made rock quarry that has been filled in with water can provide such an environment. Quarries can have areas that are over 100 feet deep and are used for a variety of SCUBA diving certification classes. The benefit of a quarry is that the environment is relatively stable without the hindrance of tides and currents. Keep in mind that you will be less buoyant in fresh water than you will be in salt water so your weights will have to be adjusted accordingly. If you want to test your newly learned skills at greater depths and continue to push yourself to go farther, a quarry is a great place to train.

Whenever practicing diving skills in water, it is ultra important to use a buddy. Even if you are in the shallow end of a swimming pool or your bathtub, if you pass out in four inches of water you will be in serious trouble without someone watching over you. When you have a buddy present you can really push your own limits while staying safe in any body of water.

Out of air – time to come up

When you practice holding your breath out of the water, it's pretty easy to push yourself really far. It's not so scary because even if the worst thing possible happened and you lost consciousness, you will not drown and die. Your body's automatic controls would take over and while knocking your brain unconscious it would start to breathe. If this happens underwater – forget about it.

If you've been doing some dry land breath hold training up until this point you may have noticed that there is a time toward the end of your breath that your body starts to get pretty uncomfortable. You get anxious and jittery and you feel the pressures of your body's automatic controls trying to take over. As you fight it with your mind the urge to breathe gets stronger and stronger. Fighting it more at this point may cause you to start to have some involuntary contractions or convulsions. When you are dry, see how far you can push yourself beyond this crazy uncomfortable phase of your breath hold. This is the point at which a normal person would just give up, let it all out and start to breathe. But you are a spearfisherman in training. You have signed up for one of the most dangerously exciting activities that a human being can physically do. You are putting your body to the test and pushing its limits beyond anything it has done before. You are also learning. Each time you practice this and know how the contractions feel, you will also begin to know that they will pass and that you will be able to mentally control them so they do not control you.

Your body has a reserve oxygen supply that is ready and waiting for you when you need it. The contractions are the first hint that your body is planning to tap into the reserves. This is the mental game. If you can trust the fact that you still have a decent amount of oxygen left after the contractions start, then you can train your mind to know that this is merely a phase that you need to get through. This is also why it is important to do a significant amount of dry training. The more you do this and experience what it feels like to be very low on air, the better prepared you will be for when it happens to you underwater. You will know when you still have a few more seconds down below and you will know when it is ultimately time to come back up.

When it is time to come up you will be happy to know that the pressure you have been equalizing during your entire descent will now be working in your favor. Going up will cause all of the air spaces within you to expand. Your ears will naturally release the expanding air with no need to equalize like before. Your lungs will expand with whatever remaining air is left in them and as this happens you will feel a sense of having a bit more time in your breath hold. This is pretty amazing because you suddenly go from a very uncomfortable feeling of being out of breath at the bottom, to a fairly relieved feeling that you will make it to the surface in time.

When coming up from a fairly deep dive (greater than 30 feet) another pretty cool thing happens as a result of the change in pressure. We talked about mask squeeze in an earlier section so think about a mask squeeze in reverse. While going down we had to give up a little bit of our stored air to our mask's air space as it was being compressed. Well, that compressed space is now expanding like a balloon as you head to the surface. Normally, after that space fills to maximum capacity and continues to expand, the air would then find its way out by breaking a tiny seal in the rubber skirt of your mask. This usually goes unnoticed as there isn't any pain or discomfort from a slight leak of air out of a mask. However, as we get smarter and more experienced we will make use of this expanding air before it has a chance to escape us.

The expanding air within our mask space has given us a little gift. The gift is a mini breath. While diving down we gave up a small amount of air to counteract the mask squeeze but while rising up we get to steal it back. If we don't, it will be lost out the side of our mask so we might as well take advantage of this little gift and use it to help get back to the surface safely and more comfortably.

As you feel the expansion of the air within your mask it will actually start to lift away from your face. At this point, simply take a small puff of a breath in through your nose until your mask squeezes firmly around your face again. It's really an oddly phenomenal feeling when you suddenly get the satisfaction of even the slightest bit of air again. When used correctly, this mini breath will help get you back to the surface even when you think you have stayed down below a bit past your comfort level. Depending on your depth, you may be able to get more than one mini breath as the pressure continues to expand the air in your mask as you ascend.

Pushing your body past its limits is an exercise best suited for out of the water. Ultimately you will be training and testing limits in the water and this is one of those things that can only be done at significant depth. Use the mini breath as a tool but be smart and don't completely rely on it.

Warning – The shallow water blackout

When you finish a long dive and are almost at the top, you will get a huge sense of relief by blowing all of your remaining air out of your mouth. Time this right so you will be ready to take a big breath of fresh air in as you burst through the surface of the water. This is the point where science and knowledge can mean the difference between life and death for the freediver. When you put your body through the stresses of breath holding to the max, upon completion of a dive there is an abundance of CO_2 in your system and a sudden drop in blood pressure. If these two things are not addressed, you run the risk of possibly blacking out at the surface.

The shallow water blackout, also known in the diving community as a 'samba,' is the number one most frightening thing that could happen to a spearfisherman. Yes, even scarier than sharks! The overwhelming majority of blackouts occur right at the point when the diver breaches the surface and in the following 30 seconds or less. This is because the physiologic changes happening within the body have not been respected and corrected. A sudden drop in blood pressure can cause fainting even if it happens in the process of standing up quickly after lying flat for a while on your couch at home. In order to regulate your blood pressure and purge any excess CO_2

in your system, it is vitally important to learn how to properly breathe when you breach the surface.

Once again there is no real substitute for professional dive instruction when it comes to this matter. In my training I was taught something known as 'hook breathing' to be used as a tool at this very critical point in your dive. By altering your breathing for the first six breaths after surfacing, you will vastly reduce your chances of a shallow water blackout during the phase of the dive that it is most likely to occur.

Hook breathing, a term used to describe these recovery breaths, consists of a big breath in followed by a 3 second hold of the breath before releasing it. The purpose of this is to begin to build your blood pressure up again after a sudden drop. Repeat this hook breathing cycle three times – taking a big breath in and holding for a few seconds before finally releasing.

The next three breaths are designed to get the CO_2 out and a new flow of oxygen in. Take a big breath in, followed by an immediate big breath out - three consecutive times. Once this six breath series is complete, you can go back to normal breathing. As long as you feel fine and not disoriented during the next 30 seconds you will most likely be out of danger.

Hook Breathing Cycle
- Big inhalation, hold (3 seconds), release
- Big inhalation, hold (3 seconds), release
- Big inhalation, hold (3 seconds), release

Purge Breaths
- Big inhalation, immediate big exhalation
- Big inhalation, immediate big exhalation
- Big inhalation, immediate big exhalation

In addition to helping yourself through this potentially dangerous period, this is where a dive buddy can prove most valuable. When you have a buddy waiting for you at the surface he can help to guide you through these learned breathing patterns even if you feel slightly disoriented. Your buddy is your safety net and the moment you think you don't need one any longer is the moment that your new hobby becomes very dangerous.

Chapter 7 – Underwater Hunting

A stealthy approach

It's time to catch some fish and in order to do that you will have to channel your inner predator. The fish that you are targeting live in the wild they are pre-programmed to be ultra cautious. Danger and death lurks around every corner and they have to rely on their natural instincts to stay alive. Your only advantage is your superior intellect which has enabled human beings to dominate the planet and rise to the top of the food chain. Modern society has suppressed much of our inherent killer instinct so it is up to you to figure out how to get back in touch with your primal side.

The first thing to remember, which should come as no surprise, is to remain as stealthy and quiet as possible. I have been preaching calmness and relaxation from the beginning. Not only is this important in order to get your heart rate down and to conserve energy but it is equally important in order to get close to the fish. Fish will get nervous if you make a lot of noise and unnecessary movements and they will make themselves scarce. If you hug the bottom, act like a rock and keep calm, you will find that the fish will come to you. As long as you choose a location that satisfies the requirements of an environment that should hold fish, they will come to you.

Another thing to consider is the noise that your equipment is making. Sound travels much faster underwater and the littlest noise can be magnified significantly. A speargun made of wood compared to metal can reduce sounds made from objects clinking together. Loose clips, cables, buckles, straps and cords can all make strange sounds compared to the natural underwater environment. You will even hear the squeaking of your wetsuit from rubbing rubber as it is amplified so do your best to sound as natural as possible. Be aware of your sounds and make adjustments to your equipment to minimize anything that is out of the ordinary.

Stick to the bottom

The sea bottom is the fish super highway. The majority of the time, this is the place to be as productive as possible. As you increase your bottom times you will also increase your chances of success. We've reviewed a variety of fish species and each of them have their own degree of comfort with strangers in their midst. Almost universally though, if you hold to the bottom and stay quiet, all of these fish will come to you.

If you find yourself a bit underweighted, you may have the tendency to float up off the bottom or struggle to stay there without moving. The obvious solution to this is to add more weight. However, if you are in shallow water, excess weight may be too uncomfortable at the surface. In situations like these you may want to do a quick scan of the bottom for some type of structure that you can hold onto. I will sometimes dive down and if I find myself starting to float I will grab the nearest rock with my free hand and use that to keep me pinned down. In sandy bottom situations I have scooped my free hand under the sand and used that as my anchor. It doesn't take much but it is important so that you don't have to struggle and lose your focus on staying cool, calm and comfortable.

Line up your shot

As the fish start to appear in your sights it will be tempting at first to shoot anything within range. Gathering information about the fish in your particular area will help you to make smart decisions when it comes to spearfishing. Most game fish have size, bag and season limits that must be respected at all times. This information is usually available online on your particular state's division of fish and game website.

For example, if I am targeting striped bass, I need to know that in New Jersey I cannot keep a striped bass under 28 inches. Additionally, I can only keep two fish per day over 28 inches unless I have previously purchased something called a 'bonus tag' which allows me to keep a third fish that day. I also need to know that catching striped bass outside of three miles from any coastline is prohibited. You can begin to see how one particular species of fish has so many rules attached to it. Also, different states have different regulations for the same striped bass. If you plan on traveling to other states you will need to know their laws. Fortunately almost every state has their guidelines posted online for our convenience.

Assuming you have positioned yourself correctly and a striped bass swims within range, how can you tell if that fish is at least 28 inches long? Well, that is something that comes with experience. Rule of thumb is to never shoot a fish that looks even close to the minimum size limit allowed in that state. Remember that everything you see is going to be slightly magnified underwater. Because the fish you see are going to be slightly smaller than they appear, it is even more important to only target fish that look like they are well within the legal size limit. One thing that separates us from a typical rod and reel fisherman is that catch-and-release doesn't exist in spearfishing. Once we pull the trigger on a fish it had better be the right size because it won't be thrown back.

At first you will have to make an educated guess but after catching a few fish and measuring them, you will soon get accustomed to the underwater magnification factor. The underwater environment can also play tricks on your ability to judge distance as well. It would be nice to have some sort of target practice or shooting range that would help you gauge the correct distance. I suppose you could set something like that up in a swimming pool but ultimately it is going to come down to practice and experience. Start shooting at fish and soon enough you will figure out your range.

Shooting accuracy is essential. It will help you shoot more fish but more importantly, when your accuracy improves you will be able to target the vital parts of the fish. A little information on fish anatomy can go a long way when you are trying to shoot them with a spear. If you take a shot and hit a fish in a relatively soft, fleshy part of its body there is a good chance that the fish will be able to pull itself free from your spear. After being shot, all fish will struggle to quickly try to free themselves. Your spear must be placed in an area that will not easily pull free. Additionally, you don't want to shoot a hole through the meat that you will eventually be eating if it can be helped. This limits the target on most fish. The head is usually a good place to aim but it is very tempting to track a large fish by pointing at the thickest part of its body for fear of missing. Fish don't usually swim backwards so by targeting the head the fish will be more likely to swim into your kill zone if your shot is not perfect.

Fish have something called a lateral line that runs down the length of the side of their bodies about midway between the top and bottom of the fish. They use this lateral line as a super sensory organ. Most likely it is a bundle of nerves that runs along their spinal column with the function to alert the fish to any subtle environmental changes in the area. The key to this line for our purpose is to reveal to us where the spine is located. If we shoot the spine, the fish will not escape. Targeting the head is always a good idea but some fish have very hard skulls and some have very hard plates that cover their gills. If your shot is angled slightly off and hits one of these hard structures, it could deflect off the fish entirely. If you are shooting a fish that is at the maximum distance for your shooting line and spear, the point of the shaft may not have enough power to penetrate one of these hard structures. All of this information needs to be processed before taking your shot.

Fighting a fish

The location of the perfect shot is somewhere right behind the head and right along the lateral line. This shot will penetrate the spine, and almost immediately paralyze the fish. Additionally, this location will shoot a hole through the fish in an area that will minimize damage to the meat you are after. When you shoot a fish in this manner it is known as 'stoning' the fish. It basically rolls over dead right after you shoot it.

Larger fish can really make a strong surge after being shot but if you stone them – or even come close – it takes a lot of fight out of even the nastiest fish. If you miss this paralyzing shot you will be in for a fight.

The best way to handle a fish that has not been stoned is to just let it run out of steam for a while. Shoot your fish and then head to the surface for air. If you have your speargun and floatline rigged together like I do, you may need to let go of your gun for a moment while you surface. Trust in your equipment and get some air. I sometimes have to do this for larger fish but for smaller fish it is easy enough to hold onto your gun. If you feel the slightest pull from the fish, you can let go of the gun in order to prevent the fish from tearing off. You can grab hold of your floatline and let it slide through your hand while surfacing

When you get to the surface you can slowly pull your fish in toward you. Some people spearfish with guns that have reels attached to them. The purpose of the reel is to allow you to keep hold of your gun while the fish swims away – peeling line off the reel as it tries to escape. Then at the surface the fish can be fought just like a fisherman uses a rod and reel. One advantage of a reel is the security of keeping your gun in your hand. Without a reel, if you release your gun there is always the possibility of a line breaking causing you to lose your equipment. I have never used a reel and have never had the need for one. However, this decision is going to be based on the type of fish you are hunting and the situation. Large fish will require a lot more line and having a reel may be advantageous. There are ways of dealing with large fish using a float line as well so again, it will depend on your particular situation.

When you are at the surface, find your snorkel and regain your composure. It's pretty exciting when you have a nice fish on your spear but it is still important to try to remain calm. While breathing through your snorkel, grab hold of the float line and slowly bring your catch toward you. Again, if you feel resistance then give a little line back. Let the fish tire out while you slowly, methodically bring him in. There's no telling where your spear is attached at this point so you don't want to risk having it pull out by trying to land the fish too quickly. While pulling in the line it is also important to be aware of all the extra line building up around you. Do not let yourself get tangled in the line. This is especially true for very large fish like tuna. It can be dangerous if you get tangled in your line and then the fish gets a surge of life and makes a run. In a split second you can go from extreme excitement of pulling in a big fish to fighting for your life as you get pulled under water. Be mindful of all the extra line around you.

As your fish gets closer and closer to you, try to determine how good of a shot you have on your fish. If your spear is solidly attached then bring it in as quickly as you can. If not, continue to take care not to pull the spear shaft from the body of the fish. It can be a potentially dangerous situation when your fish is right next to you. The best way I have found to quickly subdue a fish is to try to hold the spear by the shaft and then find a good spot on the fish to grab. Watch out for the sharp end of the spear especially if your fish is still quite lively. As you get more experienced holding fish you will find that a firm grasp on top of the head just behind the eyes is a good location for your hand. Some toothless varieties of fish will best be handled with a grasp of the lower jaw.

Whichever way you get hold of your fish, keep it firm and don't take it off your spear until it is secured on some type of stringer. I keep a metal spike stringer attached to my float so after getting a good hold on my fish I start to pull my float toward me. Again, this puts a lot of line in the water all around your body so be careful and don't get tangled. With my float within reach I will then grab my spike stringer and poke it through the eye socket of my fish. The spike will go right through and out the other eye, securing your fish to the float. You can also spike through the lower jaw if going through the eyes is not your thing.

Next, you will have to release the fish from the spear. Sometimes, a good shot will cause the spear shaft to go completely through the fish and other times the fish will be secured with the flopper that opens after impact. Most of the time I will be pushing the entire shaft through the fish's body and out the other side in order to get it off of the spear. While doing this I know I will have to detach my shooting line from my speargun in order to pull the entire line through the fish as well. This is why I use a quick disconnect clip to attach the shooting line to the speargun. It makes it very easy to take apart and put back together whenever I put a fish on my stringer.

One word of caution if you follow the way that I secure my fish and remove the spear – when you pull the spear through the fish, take the time to reconnect it to your speargun before disconnecting the shooting line. If you don't have your spearshaft connected to anything there is a chance that you could accidentally drop your spear in the process of detaching lines and holding onto everything else. This happened to me one time and I watched my spear sink into the darkness below as I floated on the surface. In murky water there is virtually no chance of recovering a dropped spear unless you are extremely lucky. When that happens to you, it is a very memorable mistake to learn from. Without a spear, my day of fishing was over. This is yet another reason to have some spare equipment with you if possible. While spearfishing from a boat you may have the advantage of storing such things on board.

Another thing worth mentioning while immobilizing a speared fish is the use of a dive knife. Some fish that are particularly lively need to be dispatched so they don't impose any danger to you. If you carry a dive knife like many spearfishermen do, you can use your knife to kill the fish quickly. Many people push the point of a knife into the top of the head of the fish into its brain. Another way is to 'bleed' your fish by either poking a hole into the side of your fish just behind the pectoral fin – or by cutting the gills. Cutting through any major artery will cause the fish to quickly bleed out. On some species it will be advantageous to bleed your fish in order to prevent contamination of the meat by the blood of a dying fish. This holds true for most fast moving fish such as tuna and other pelagics. It is worth taking the time to bleed these fish in order to immobilize them and to care for the meat.

Personally, I choose not to carry a knife on my body while spearfishing. With a thrashing fish in the midst I do not want to risk a potential knife accident. Whenever you can prevent a possible accident by being smart and being careful it will be in your best interest. On the flip side, there are situations where a knife could save your life. I had a friend who got tangled in a lobster trap line on the sea bottom one day and he was able to quickly cut himself free because he had a knife handy. You will have to decide if a knife is for you and if the benefits outweigh the potential hazards.

Reloading

Taking a fish off your spear and securing it on your float stringer takes quite a bit of time and effort. More importantly it drains a lot of your stamina and energy. Catching a fish is very exciting and it gets your adrenaline flowing and your heart pumping. This physiologic change is very helpful during the process of securing your catch but when that's over and it's time to get back on the hunt, you will need to start conserving your energy again. Take your time putting your speargun, spear and shooting line back together. It will take a lot of effort to pull on those power bands again. I usually fish with three bands and I know it will drain me to reload all three. Do this slowly. Take your time, breathe deep and slow and start the process of getting your heart rate back to normal.

It's easy to get excited when you know there are fish in the area. After catching one it is natural to want to get right back to it as quickly as possible. If you rush through the reloading step and don't take time to regulate your breathing, your very next dive will be a very short one. There's nothing more frustrating than running out of air when there are fish around. The more you try to get underwater quickly, the shorter your dives will be. Remember that the reloading phase takes time and effort and there's just no way around it. The fish will still be there so take your time to gather yourself prior to diving down.

After you have your power bands reloaded just lay on the surface nice and still and breathe. Remember your recovery breathing cycles and start from the beginning again.

Recovery/Relaxation Breathing Cycle
1. Inhale (3-4 seconds)
2. Hold (2 seconds)
3. Exhale (10 seconds)
4. Hold (2 seconds)
5. Repeat for your desired number of cycles

After you have completed your cycles and feel like you are ready to shoot some more fish, do a few purge breaths to release excess CO_2. Breathe easy for a couple seconds and then take your one big breath in before diving under.

If you find that your dive following the capture of a fish is a relatively short one, there's a good chance that you did not recover long enough at the surface. Take your time and do it again. Check your dive watch and pay close attention to your surface interval time. Make sure that any subsequent surface intervals are at least twice as long as your previous dive. Fundamentals and patience will pay off so do not rush to get back underwater too quickly.

Keeping a log

As you start to gain proficiency and experience in your new hobby you may find it helpful to keep a record of your underwater encounters. Fishermen routinely keep logs of their catches that include specific details about species, location, time, tide, weather, wind, bait, tackle, etc. Fish are instinctively creatures of habit and go through cycles that can repeat year after year. Some fish are migratory and some stay in an area year round. If you live in an area like I do where the seasons dramatically change each year you will definitely notice significant changes to the ecosystems.

When I lived in Rhode Island I would follow a similar pattern each year that would begin with winter flounder fishing in March. Then in April the herring would spawn and make a run up certain rivers to find fresh water. This triggered an early spring striped bass bite. In May there would be a massive migration of squid into the back bay to mate. Again, the striped bass would surge during this time due to the abundance of food available. In June, as the weather started to warm, we would see more bluefish and the fluke would start to inhabit the inshore waters. On and on it would go. Each month would seemingly bring in a new wave of fish based on either migratory or mating patterns. You need to study these patterns in order to know what to target at any particular time of year.

I made a point to keep a spearfishing logbook with details and photos whenever I went out. It is still helpful to look back on such a log and use that information as a guide each time I go. The more information you accumulate the better chance you will have of being successful by following the patterns that you have personally witnessed in the past. Certain locations and certain species of fish can be quite predictable – although there are always new surprises waiting for you out there as well.

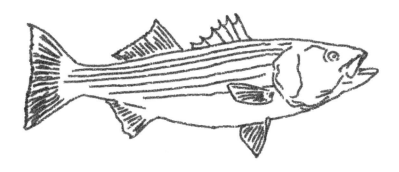

Chapter 8 - Caring For Your Catch

Ice Bath

If you are like me, your underlying goal in spearfishing is to catch some fish for the dinner table. I don't like to waste any of the fish that I catch and that is why it is ultra important to know how to properly care for it. If treated properly, fresh fish can last about a week without freezing any of it.

The first step, which we already discussed, is bleeding your fish. Some fish do not require bleeding but if it does, this will need to be done while the fish is still alive and kicking. Bleed a fish immediately so that the still beating heart can pump as much blood out as possible before the fish dies. Once dead, it will be impossible to bleed your fish.

The next and possibly most important step is to get that fish icy cold as quickly as possible. A quick deep chill will do wonders to keep a fish fresh for a long time. Conversely, if your fish dies and is tossed into a bin with other dead fish the flesh will start to degrade very quickly. It's even worse if the fish is left out in the heat. Don't let all of your efforts go to waste by not properly caring for your catch.

An effective way of chilling your catch is to come prepared with an ice chest or cooler full of ice. This is pretty easy if you are spearfishing from a boat but not so simple from a shore or kayak dive. In a situation where you do not have a cooler nearby, keep your fish attached to your stringer, floating in the water it came from. When you call it quits for the day, make it a high priority to get your fish into ice as soon as possible.

To go a step further, take a bucket full of seawater and dump it into your cooler of ice cubes to form an ice slurry. The salt content in the water will super-chill the slurry and enable you to cool the flesh of the fish very quickly. The additional water will completely surround the fish leaving no air space between ice cubes. The cold will prevent the degradation of the meat and keep it well preserved for a very long time. In addition it will help to firm up the flesh and prevent moisture loss when you are cleaning and cooking your fish. There are many advantages of quickly chilling your freshly caught fish so a little forethought and preparation will go a long way.

Brine is a salt water solution that is used in many forms of cooking in order to prevent moisture loss and enhance flavor in meats and fish. It has become common practice to brine a Thanksgiving turkey for this purpose. By submerging meat into a saturated salt water solution the muscle tissue undergoes a molecular change. Brine can also include sugar, herbs and spices but the salt, in particular, causes the protein fibers within the meat to denature. This has the effect of locking in moisture by preventing its escape through the muscle cell membrane. I am not going to get into any more chemistry beyond this but just remember that a super cold, salty water bath for your catch will keep it fresh and firm for a long time and keep it moist and delicious after cooking.

Cleaning

There is some controversy about when to clean, butcher or fillet your fish after catching it. I have a certain opinion about this and I will share my ideas and explain why I do the things I do. Hopefully it will make sense and justify the time and effort it takes to properly care for your catch. I am not going to get into the how-to's of filleting other than to say that a long, sharp, flexible fillet knife is a great tool to own. This section is going to be more about the preparation and preservation of fresh fish in order to minimize waste and to get the most out of your catch.

We have just reviewed all of the benefits of a super cooled ice bath immediately after catching your fish. To expand on that one step further, I prefer to keep my fish in this slurry for 24 hours, or at least overnight. I feel as if this extended stay in the ice water really helps to firm up the flesh of the fish and not only does this have some culinary benefits but it also makes filleting the fish a lot easier and cleaner. When the fish is chilled it does not bleed at all when you cut into the flesh. It is also easier to contain the fluids that reside within the organ systems and stomach cavity because this too is chilled. I find it very important to not contaminate the meat by letting it touch blood or organ fluid. If you are careful not to puncture into the stomach area with your knife you can prevent this.

I try to keep all excess moisture off my fish fillets - even to the extreme of not washing fresh fillets with water after cleaning. Again, if you are careful and do not contaminate the meat then a fresh fillet should only require a light pat down with a paper towel. If I plan to cook the fish at a later date I will wrap it in paper towel and store it in a covered bin in the refrigerator. Most fresh fillets will keep like this for several days.

Too often, fishermen will fillet their catch soon after the fishing is over. Sometimes this is out of necessity in order to divide the catch between several people. Hopefully the fish was chilled in a cooler full of ice shortly after being caught. However, by cleaning too soon the flesh has not had proper time to cure and firm up. Fillets are usually soft and contaminated with other fluids like blood, bile and slime. If you must fillet your fish immediately, the next best way to preserve your catch is to clean it in cold, fresh water and then submerge it in a brine such as a salt and water mixture. After brining for a few hours, rinse off the solution with fresh water and then thoroughly dry the fillets with paper towels before refrigerating. Store fillets dry in a container in the refrigerator. If even more chilling is desired you can fill some zip top bags with ice cubes and salt and keep your fillets on top of the bag. Super cold (just below freezing) and dry are the two keys to preserving fish as long as possible.

I learned a lot about preserving clean, fresh fish by talking to many sushi chefs over the years. As you can imagine, if people are going to be eating their fish raw it will have to be as clean as possible. The quality and texture of the flesh is also taken very seriously by experienced sushi chefs. Very rarely is the fish at a sushi bar completely frozen. Most likely it is kept in a super chilled state from the boat to the plate. Some exceptions to this are when it is possible to flash freeze a product in order to kill potentially harmful bacteria or to transport a catch over very long distances. Extreme care is taken in sushi restaurants to keep the fish as fresh as possible for obvious reasons.

Several sushi bar conversations have taught me about the importance of putting a fresh catch on ice as soon as possible and not cutting into the fish until the following day. After using this tip for several species of fish, I have concluded that it yields the cleanest possible result. So much, in fact, that I have been able to eat many fish that I have caught, in the same style as they are served in a sushi bar – raw. I would be very hesitant to do this with fish prepared any other way or fish that has been in contact with bodily fluids.

Preserving

If sushi isn't your thing and you just plan to cook your fish, you will still benefit from all of the cleaning methods previously described. I would encourage people to never freeze fish because I think it has a negative effect on the taste and texture. The longer it stays in the freezer, the more the quality drops. Any air that is surrounding a frozen piece of fish will cause it to degrade and eventually get freezer burn.

If you absolutely must freeze your catch it is important to try to eliminate as much air as possible around your fish. The best way that I have been able to accomplish this is to use a device designed to vacuum the air out of a freezer bag and seal the bag so that no more air can get in. There are several products on the market that can do this adequately. With a vacuum seal, frozen fish will keep pretty well preserved for several weeks. It is not indestructible though. I have eaten fish that has been sealed and frozen for up to 6 months but there is a distinct drop in quality compared to fresh. If you do freeze fish this way, it would be best to be eaten within a couple weeks from catching it to minimize degradation.

A good quality vacuum sealing device can cost over $100 but if you catch a great deal of fish and are unable to eat it all right away, this cost can be well justified. The device can also be used for a wide variety of other food products such as meats, cheeses, vegetables, etc. Due to its ability to multitask I think a vacuum sealer would be a worthy appliance to have in any household.

Chapter 9 – Specialty Hunting

Diving at night

The underwater realm is a mysterious and unique environment. I see something interesting and different every time I make a new dive. Sometimes it can be quite surprising – you really never know what you are going to come face to face with when you enter this world. Hopefully it's nothing dangerous but that possibility also exists.

Things won't seem so mysterious once you get accustomed to diving in a particular area. Every now and then however, something new will pop up and catch your interest. I remember seeing a porcupine puffer fish for the first time in an area I least expected it. This is certainly a very distinct creature and one you will not likely forget. They are quite docile and will allow you to swim right up to them – sometimes close enough to touch. I suppose it's because they have all of those spines to protect them. I think they may also be venomous as well so it's best to keep your distance.

Squid are also very interesting to see in their natural habitat. They have these big curious eyes and look right at you but they are fairly weary and tend to keep their distance. Squid also have the ability to change colors in an instant and swim backward just as easily as forward. And don't get too close because if you do – poof! – they will shoot out a protective cloud of ink. These are just a few of the millions of odd and unique creatures that you may someday encounter while diving.

As amazing and mysterious as the underwater environment is during the day, it's a whole new ballgame at night. I would advise a new diver by saying that you should be extremely comfortable diving during the day before venturing into the water at night. The first few times going night diving is a mental shock to the system and if you are unprepared, it can be a bit overwhelming.

The first time I had an opportunity to dive at night was when a new friend of mine introduced me to lobster diving. I was very excited about the prospect of catching lobster – especially grabbing them by hand while freediving. This is about as adventurous as it gets. My heightened adrenaline got me through the tough part which was just getting acclimated to the water at night.

Prior to our dive, my friend Dave did the best he could to describe the process of lobster hunting. He was experienced and was anxious to be my mentor. Dave told me about the best underwater dive light available at the time. It was called the Light Cannon 100 and although it was fairly expensive, he assured me that the price was well worth it. I picked one up at a local dive shop along with a lobster gauge. The gauge is used to measure your lobsters to make sure you are only taking the ones above the legal size limit. There are very tight restrictions on lobster harvesting and very harsh punishments for those who do not follow the rules. Other than a light and a gauge there are really no other pieces of specialized equipment necessary to catch lobsters. Although you may spend a bit for a quality light, with your basic freediving equipment you should be ready for lobster. I also found it helpful on a few occasions to have on board a good supply of spare batteries for the dive light. Just like having spare speargun parts, an extra set of batteries can mean the difference between a successful dive or a bust.

Dave told me that the basic idea was to dive to the bottom, search around rock piles for lobsters, shine your light in the lobster's face and reach around to grab it by the back. This seemed easy enough in theory. I had thick neoprene gloves. How hard could it be?

This was a boat dive and I was invited aboard his vessel for my first night dive. After arriving at our location (which was a long rock wall jetty) we geared up and were prepared to jump in. Dave went in first and prompted me to follow. I had never jumped into the water in the dark before and I had a whole bunch of mixed emotions about it. Thankfully we were not in the ocean but rather in a back bay area. This put most of my sharky thoughts to rest – not all of them, but most. Dave started swimming away from me and I gathered up my courage to jump in. When I hit the water, I'll never forget my initial experience of splashing into an area full of seemingly invisible jellyfish. These were the harmless, clear, round jellies that are common to the bay. You don't even see them during the day because the light goes right through them. At night however, when these jellyfish are touched they give off a natural bioluminescence and you see a flicker of neon green light. This totally took me by surprise when all of a sudden I plunged into the water and all I could see was flickering green light everywhere I turned.

I have had some experience with these jellyfish in the past so it wasn't a complete shock. And speaking of shocks, I knew enough to remember that these were not a stinging variety of jellyfish. After getting past the field of jellies I turned on my light and found out why it was so aptly named the Light Cannon. I had a nicely lit path in front of me now and I was headed toward the rocks. In my light beam I started to see so many little particles and organisms teeming with life. Tiny baitfish even started to corral around me as they were attracted to my light source. Without my light it was pitch black. With the light I was in an ecosystem the likes of which I had never seen before. It was really fascinating and a bit spooky at the same time.

It took some time to get adjusted to all of my new surroundings but after I did, it was business as usual in the world of diving. I knew that I had to get my breathing under control and I also knew that this mental over-stimulation would have my heart pounding and my adrenaline flowing. I needed to get in control and the best way to do this would be to start some recovery breathing cycles - back to the basics. Whenever you find yourself a bit over stimulated, it's a good idea to remember your fundamentals and get back to the basics.

When it was finally time to make my first dive, my light would lead the way all the way to the bottom which was about 20 feet down. Although slightly scary due to the inability to see anything that wasn't in the path of the light beam, this wasn't all that different from daytime spearfishing. In the daylight with a mask on, you can't see in back of your head and your peripheral vision is also significantly limited. At night it's just a matter of moving your light wherever you pivot your head.

Even with this powerful light, in my area the water visibility doesn't clear up until you are about six feet from the bottom. As you dive down through the murk, all of a sudden the shapes of rocks and other bottom structures that are familiar start to come into view. That is the reason I made the point earlier about the importance of having a particular level of comfort, experience and confidence of daytime diving before tackling the night. Even on my very first night dive, I had the general knowledge of my area so I had some idea about what to expect when I reached the bottom.

What I didn't expect was the whole host of other life forms that are usually dormant during the day but come out at night. In addition, many of the fish that are quite active during the day find shelter and seemingly go to sleep at night. This may not be the same sleep that you and I are accustomed to. After all, fish can't even close their eyes. With the possibility of predators nearby, it wouldn't be a good idea to close your eyes anyway. Although fish may appear to sleep, most likely they are just in some kind of dormant shut down mode during the night. Of course this makes them easy to sneak up on – especially if you have a blinding light to shine on them. Ever hear of 'deer in the headlights?' Well, the same principle applies to fish and lobster.

I may not recall my very first lobster encounter but I do remember that the lobsters would not usually be out in the open making themselves easy pickings for the likes of me. And I learned very quickly that lobsters in the wild absolutely do not come with those big fat rubber bands around their claws. Most of the time, when I would spot a lobster it was sitting with its tail and body backed into some type of cave or crevasse in a rock pile with the business end sticking out into the open. Reflecting on my mentor's instructions I was supposed to shine my light into the lobster's face and then reach around with my free hand and grab its back. So how do you do this when a lobster is backed into a cave? Well, there comes a time in the career of every lobster hunter when you have to decide if your neoprene gloves are thick enough to protect you from a head on attack. If you are going to catch a lobster backed into a hole, there's only one way in and there's a good chance that he's going to disagree with your plan of attack.

This is what makes it exciting! It's you, pitted up against the lobster - one on one. No weapons other than your hands and light versus his claws and survival instincts. You have one breath to get it done. Decide. Are you going to stick your hand right into that hole and right into those claws? Or are you going to chicken out? One breath. Time is running out.

Many times I have taken that dare and have won. Many times I have come out with just a single claw in my hand. And many times I have lost – either getting clawed in the process or because the lobster had an escape route out the back of his hole. With one swift flick of its strong tail, a lobster can swim completely out of reach. There have also been many occasions where I end up chasing after the lobster as it scoots from rock to rock trying to escape. Unlike fish, a lobster tires rather quickly and because it has to propel itself backwards by flipping its tail, I don't know how it has any idea where it's headed while frantically being chased. Chasing lobsters expends a lot of energy and oxygen so once that starts, your breath will diminish rapidly.

Ideally, when you spot a lobster with your light it will be walking around out in the open. They are nocturnal creatures and tend to be more active at night so seeing them outside of their protective shelter is somewhat common. These are the lobsters that you can sneak up on. Just as Dave taught, shine your light directly at the lobster and as you get closer, prepare to reach around to grab its back shell before it realizes what is happening. Watch out for those claws. Get a good grip and hang on while swimming the lobster to the surface.

It is rare that you would be able to grab multiple lobsters on any particular dive but there will be circumstances where you may see more than one at a time. Choosing either the largest or the one you have the best chance at capturing is usually a good strategy. Trying to grab more than one, usually ends up in getting none. If you are in a particularly productive area it may be a good idea to take a lobster bag along with you as you dive. That way you can grab one and put it in your bag while you attempt to get another. When I dive for lobsters I still use my regular floatline but instead of attaching it to my speargun, I attach one end to my dive belt and the other end to a tube floating at the surface. My tube has a mesh net in the center so when I bring up a lobster I can toss it right in. I also keep my lobster measuring gauge attached to my float in order to measure any lobsters that are questionable in size. If they are undersized it is your obligation to release that lobster immediately back to the water it came from.

On my very first lobster dive with Dave, I was proud of myself for capturing one keeper size lobster. I had a few other smaller ones that were thrown back. All in all it was an exciting first encounter with the creatures of the night. Dave came back with about eight so I knew it was possible and I would use this experience as a stepping stone to future trips. It was great to have a teacher along with me to help me realize that many of the potentially frightening things were actually quite normal.

After going a few times with Dave, I had the confidence to then pass the knowledge that I had acquired down to some of my friends. I became the mentor and it was interesting to witness how each new person reacted to diving at night for the first time. Even after going several times there were occasionally things that would surprise me. I'll always remember one particular night dive in pretty murky water. I did everything I normally do in pre-dive preparation. As I began my descent in about 20 feet of water I could barely see my hand in front of my face. The water was just very cloudy and I was hoping it would clear up as I got closer to the bottom. It finally did, but there was only about two feet of clarity off the bottom and when I broke through the murk I arrived in an area that I like to call "Spider Crab City." Spider crabs are virtually harmless but if you have ever seen one up close, face to face, they are not the most welcoming creatures around. I encounter them quite often while spearfishing but usually pay little attention to them. They are not edible (by my standards) and they are very ugly looking – almost pre-historic. On this particular lobster dive I came through the dark cloudy water to arrive at the bottom up close and personal with about 50 big spider crabs! My body could barely fit between the layer of murkiness and a bottom blanketed with spider crabs. It shocked me so much that I immediately lost my breath and had to surface. It was just too freaky.

Spearfishing at night

After going lobster diving several times at night there were many times that I had wished that I had my speargun handy. On one occasion I came face to face with a very large striped bass. Presumably, it was doing the same thing I was – hunting for lobsters. Lobsters are a favorite food of striped bass and I have pulled them from the bellies of bass on numerous occasions while cleaning them. The rock piles where lobsters are frequently found also give protection to blackfish. I have witnessed many sleeping blackfish while searching for lobsters and it would have been nice to have my spear.

Sometimes you just have to choose one thing or the other. Carrying a speargun while diving for lobsters can be a bit cumbersome. It can interfere with your ability to chase them down. I suppose you could fire off a shot at an escaping lobster but I don't recommend shooting anywhere near rocks. With one hand occupied holding the light and the other holding a speargun, you are left without a hand to catch a lobster.

Just remember that there may be opportunities to spear fish at night and it wouldn't hurt to have a speargun or at bare minimum some type of pole spear available on board your boat. You never know what you will encounter so it's always smart to be as prepared as possible.

Chapter 10 – Spearfishing Tournaments

I am not going to say too much about spearfishing tournaments other than to let you know that they exist and how they basically work. Similar to the many varieties of derbies or tournaments in the world of sport fishing, spearfishing enthusiast have developed a series of their own competitions. The way fishing tournaments usually work is that prizes are awarded to contestants for specific achievements. A certain number of contestants pay an entry fee in order to participate. The event is scheduled for a particular day or maybe even spread over a longer time period depending on the rules set forth by the organizers of the tournament. There is a specific start time and a specific end time. One popular example of a fishing tournament is simply to award a prize to the person who catches the biggest fish. There are endless numbers of other variables that can also award a contestant with a prize such as: longest fish, heaviest fish, most fish, most weight, most fish species, largest fish of a particular species, etc. Heck, I've even witnessed fishing tournaments with an award for the cutest fish!

Spearfishing contests that I have seen work in a pretty interesting way. Points are awarded for every different species of fish that you land and additional points are given for either the weight of the fish or the length of the fish. Basically you are trying to get the largest fish you can in all of the possible species of fish available. The catch is that once you land a particular species, you are not supposed to shoot another fish of that species – even if it is larger than the one previously landed. For obvious reasons, this rule is in place in order to prevent the unnecessary killing of fish. The same rules and regulations about state legal size limits also apply and in tournaments the size limits are sometimes elevated in an effort to make sure that small fish are not killed.

At the end of the tournament there is usually a predetermined location for the contest authorities to do a weigh-in. Contestants gather around to show off their achievements and to find out who has done the best. Prizes are awarded in several categories and the majority of the fish that are brought in are donated to a local food bank or other needy charitable organization. In many tournaments the contestants will all gather together at the conclusion in order to socialize and share information about the day.

A spearfishing tournament is a great opportunity for someone new to the sport to learn from people who have gathered a tremendous amount of experience over the years. The social event at the end may offer you the chance to ask questions, learn about different equipment, see lots of different fish and maybe even find out about some new locations to try. Some people are against spearfishing tournaments claiming that they promote a lot of needless killing. Even if you do not participate in a particular tournament, it is not a bad idea to visit the event in an effort to gain information about the sport. As much as you think you may know, there is always something you can still learn. Have an open mind, gather information when it's available and always keep moving forward.

Spearfishing

How to Get Started

Doug Peterson

Appendix A - Online spearfishing resources

leisurepro.com
Leisure Pro - the online diver emporium. If they don't have it here, it might not exist.

makospearguns.com
Mako Spearguns – this is a fantastic site for all things related to spearfishing. Great prices and products.

deeperblue.com
Deeper Blue Forums: The World's Largest Community Dedicated to Freediving, Scuba Diving and Spearfishing – This is an online gathering place to share information with people from all over the world. A fantastic resource for new spearfishermen.

eliossub.com
Elios is known worldwide for their custom skin-diving wetsuits.

suunto.com
Suunto – watches for outdoor enthusiasts. Look for their latest freediving computer.

amazon.com
Amazon – online retailer. Not dive specific but this superstore may have what you need at a discounted price.

freedivenyc.com
Freedive NYC is a great resource to get some high quality training from certified dive instructors. If you live in the vicinity of NY, NJ, PA or CT, contact this group and take one of their weekend courses. If you live outside this area, simply search online for 'freediving instruction' for a course near you

Index

basic equipment, 23
  checklist, 102
  cost, 57
  dive computer, 54
  dive float, 52
  dive light, 56, 144
  fins, 42
  floatline, 50
  flopper, 47
  fogging, 38
  knife, 55
  mask, 33
  power bands, 48
  shooting line, 47
  snorkel, 39
  spear, 47
  speargun, 44
  stringer, 55
  underwater camera, 55
  weight belt, 30
  wetsuits, 24
boat, 92
breathing, recovery, 109
buddy system, 20
buoyancy, 16
cleaning fish, 140
equalizing, 13, 115

fish
  blackfish, 75
  bluefish, 79
  fluke, 77
  other, 83
  porgy, 81
  striped bass, 72
  triggerfish, 82
formula for success, 7
freediving, 8
GPS, 67, 93
gun loading, 105
hook breathing, 125
kayak, 89
ladder, 101
lobsters, 144
log book, 136
night diving, 144
reloading, 135
SCUBA dive certification, 5
shallow water blackout, 20, 124
sinus infection, 15
structure, 66
tournaments, 151
vacuum sealing, 142

Made in the USA
San Bernardino, CA
08 July 2018